ACCLAIM FOR *INVOKI*

'*Invoking Ireland* is a miscellany of parables an
individuals, and not as a herd, we might find a way of living authentically
on this island ... Moriarty writes a prose poetry in whose doorways we
can discern the shades of William Yeats and Dylan Thomas, David Jones
and Jack Yeats. Who else but Moriarty could combine in his palette the
voices of Blathmac and Traherne?

Moriarty's conversation is a dialogue between Christianity and pre-
Celtic Ireland. If there is a saving evolutionary, environmental moment,
it is what the painters of the Renaissance saw: that when, in Gethsemane,
the disciples fall asleep, Christ stays awake. *Invoking Ireland* is an elucida-
tion of Patrick Kavanagh's prayer: "We must be nothing/Nothing that
God may make us something."

Strange to surmise that in twenty years from now ... one will see in
TCD under the severe, genial eye of Bishop Berkeley the new John Moriarty Chair of Wisdom Literature.' – Paul Durcan, *The Irish Times*

'Moriarty's work is written with a glorious innocence and a knowing wisdom, ranging between superb storytelling and rhetorical flourishes, and it
would be my dream that everyone would read this book, take its truths to
heart, and take from Irish society the harshness of the legacy we are cur-
rently bequeathing to a sorry future.' – John F. Deane, *Irish Independent*

'*Invoking Ireland* is a collection of commentaries on various folktales and
mythic stories which have had relevance for Irish people over the centuries ... It is a whirlwind of powerful imaginative prose. Moriarty is a
writer who, over a number of significant works, has been trying to tell us
that we are capable of being awake in a deeper, more visceral and more
potent way than merely by thinking thoughts.

As we gaze into the misty realms of Irish mythology, he wants to
undress our mind of its reason, and plunge it into a sense of being which
transcends ego-ic parameters. He wants us to share his exploration of Irish
myth at this deep psychological level, so that we can find new meaning in
the old stories, and so that the old stories can bring a new perception to
the way we live out our lives.

And he succeeds so well that something new emerges. The thin line
between commentary and creative expression vanishes, and the pages of
this book deliver up extraordinary poetic thought.'
– Michael Harding, *The Sunday Tribune*

'*Invoking Ireland* takes us on a "safari of stories" around Irish mythology, and Moriarty recreates them in a way that we have never experienced them before. There is an attempt here to prod us into feeling what it was like when Aimhairghin and his pards sailed up the Kerry shore.

The original old or middle Irish poetry and tales, he quotes accurately. His translations are new and pristine and inventive. They are the kind that scholars should do if they entered into the spirit of their literature. Because it is the spirit that always inspires him, and the wrestling to make imaginative sense of what our country has said. We meet Manannán, Crom Dubh and Lugh, Christ, the Buddha and D.H. Lawrence. Dylan Thomas and Orpheus and Ted Hughes light our path or lead us into the sidings. This is a wild shaggy-haired ride along the mountains of the moon, it is a Catherine wheel of imagery, it is a great belch of the goodness of life.

Moriarty's Birdreign will never come about because we can never fly with feathered wings. We are the metallic Iron people clomping around the earth that he rails about. Life may refuse definition, but we are busy building the stockades around us. What he does magnificently is, however, to reach out and touch what it must have been like before tame philosophy, before plodding discourse, before our teeming brains straightened themselves out.

This book can only be read as mythic poetry with all its beauty and with all its roughness and with all its artlessness. It is not a book to be compromised with. It can only be embraced with fervour.'
– Alan Titley, *The Irish Book Review*

'The Ireland offered here is at once an image which subsists behind its physical appearances and an impress of all nations as inscribed in their key mythologies. Taking a line through Orphean legend, Hindu cosmology, Blake's Prophetic Books and Greek and Nordic mythology, Moriarty offers a reading of the great ongoing war between matter and spirit ... In his view, that ancient Ireland of Spirit, coherent with Nature prior to its conquest by the "cormorant tongues" of "Fomorian" man is still, potentially, realizable.

His quest, as an earlier poet put it – for Moriarty is as much poet as novelist – is to "feel back along the ancient lines of advance". But not only so. He would like to make us feel, and hear as we read, the rhythms of those ancient tongues.

John Moriarty is, I believe, a genius. If our civilization manages to survive in a form which is still capable of recognizing genius when it is pushed under its nose, it is possible, in due course, that he will be acknowledged as such.' – Robert Lumsden, *Adelaide Review*

INVOKING IRELAND
Ailiu Iath n-hErend

John Moriarty

THE LILLIPUT PRESS
DUBLIN

First published 2005 by
THE LILLIPUT PRESS
62–63 Sitric Road, Arbour Hill,
Dublin 7, Ireland
www.lilliputpress.ie

Copyright © John Moriarty, 2005, 2019

Reprinted, with corrections, 2006, 2019

The version of 'Amhairghin Glúngheal's Song' in 'Tailtiu Revisited' is by
courtesy of John Carey of University College Cork. All other copyright
acknowledgments are as detailed in the bibliography.

A CIP record for this title is available from
The British Library.

10 9 8 7 6 5 4 3

ISBN (10 DIGIT) I 84351 079 0
ISBN (13 DIGIT) 978 I 84351 079 6

Set in II.5 on I3.5pt Garamond
Printed in Poland by Drukarnia Skleniarz

CONTENTS

General Introduction

Q: Limiting yourself to a sentence or two, would you say what it is you are up to here?

A: The endeavour, such as it is, has its source in a question: how, working from within our tradition, might we reconstitute ourselves as a people?

Q: It hadn't occurred to me that we need to do any such thing.

A: The first story enacts a struggle between two peoples who have chosen two different ways of being in the world. The Fomorians have chosen to shape nature to suit them. Surrendering to it, the Tuatha Dé Danann have chosen to let nature shape them to suit it. Our way now is wholly Fomorian. It isn't working, or, rather, it has proved to be utterly disastrous; so it is that we go back out over nine waves and, wiser now we hope, we come back into an alternative experience of ourselves in a world alternatively experienced. It will make little sense to you until you have read their stories but I will say it anyway. In Fintan mac Bochra we experience ourselves alternatively in a world alternatively experienced. In Ollamh Fódhla we experience ourselves alternatively in a world alternatively experienced. And then, in one hand a beheading block and in the other an axe, a god called Cú Roí mac Daire erupts among us and all too soon we have learned that being a self of no matter what kind in a world of no matter what kind isn't the whole story. Life at the level of the subjective-objective divide, even when it is as blessed as it is in Magh Meall, isn't the final destination.

All this, and more, we mean when we sing

Ailiu Iath n-hErend

In invoking Ireland we are seeking to evoke it. In invoking it we are seeking to call it into being. And how better to call it into being than to call it into an image or archetype of itself. That image or archetype I seek neither to name nor to define, but I do seek to suggest it in a safari of stories. In our journey inland we do have to reckon with cormorant and boar and bear and badger and wolf and fox and carrion crow and hawk and stag and goat and, out of our underworld, with spectral terrors catlike in form and ferocity, all of them instinctively in ourselves as well as actually in the land. Here, in this safari into the centre, we seek to deal with them not murderously but Orphically, living with them in a great Ecumene, in Irish called In Énflaith, in English called the Birdreign.

Q: So it isn't by accident that this adventure inland begins where and when it does, in Iath nAnann at a time when two peoples are fighting for the soul of the country, one people seeking to turn it into a human convenience, the other finding fulfilment in being of one mind with the wind and the rain?

A: In the course of this battle, preoccupied as they were with it, the Tuatha Dé Danann took their eye off what is essential, and so it was that the Fomorians were able to steal their music, their very soul that is, that soul being the Orphic note that harmonized them to all things.

Q: So, in your sense of it, soul isn't a substance?

A: As I understand it here, no. Here, I think of it as a constituting disposition or attitude. Here, I think of it as a way of being oneself in a world.

Q: In that sense of soul, who or what are we now in Ireland?

A: We are Fomorians. Predominantly our collective eye is a Balar's eye, poisoned and poisoning, reducing everything in sight to commodity. And as is the collective eye so is the collective soul.

In an old account of the battle in one of Ireland's oldest books, *Cath Maige Tuiread*, is the following simple yet, in its meaning, immense sentence:

> *Tocauher a malae dia deirc Baloir.*
> Its lid was lifted off Balar's eye.

We are talking here not about its natural lid but about a multilayered, manufactured lid set in place to make sure that it didn't look at anything because anything it looked at it would destroy.

Sadly, histories of Ireland are silent about the event that has mostly driven all subsequent Irish history, the opening of what in old Irish is called the

Súil Mildagach

Concentrated though it is in one bad eye, in Balar's bad eye, it is nonetheless the collective bad eye. It is also the bad tongue, the Nemtenga, imagined here in its likeness to a cormorant's tongue and, later, in its likeness to the muscle that opens and closes a crab's claw.

So there you have it,

The *Súil Mildagach*
The Nemtenga

distinguishing us as Fomorians. It is what we have become.

Q: So, where Blake sees Urizen you see Balar?

A: Thinking of him as a collective condition, Balar is what the tradition sees.

Q: Is Balar as we find him in the Irish tradition in a way comparable to Medousa as we find her in the Greek tradition?

A: On initial inspection, there is one very obvious difference between them: whereas it is deadly to look at Medousa it is deadly to be looked at by Balar.

However, taking her myth where Greeks didn't take it, we can think of Medousa as the petra-flying principle in perception.

Whatever she looks at she turns to stone, and in this she is not unlike Balar. In that we have reduced our originally stupendous planet to economic size, we are their all too successful offspring, inheriting their ecological deadliness in instinct, eye and mind.

Q: And the remedy, if there is one?

A: Silver-branch perception, the Orphic note and the path that Jesus pioneered.

Q: What of that path?

A: Well, the thought of Jesus crossing the Torrent has left the Upanishads gasping for breath. It has left all Buddhist Sutras gasping for breath. It has left the Tao Te Ching gasping for breath. It has left the Bible speechless.

Q: Silence therefore?

A: Our tradition doesn't only know of the Súil Mildagach and the Nemtenga. Sponsored by Manannán mac Lir at sea as well as by Christ on land, it knows of In Tenga Bithnua, the ever-new tongue:

> As is the case with all other rivers, our river has its source in Connla's Well. And that is why we learn to speak. For us, to learn to speak is to learn to say:
>
> Our river has its source in the Otherworld Well.
>
> And anything we say about the hills and anything we say about the stars is a way of saying:
>
> A hazel grows over the Otherworld Well our river has its source in.
>
> Our time being so other than Otherworld time, it isn't often, in our time, that a hazelnut falls into Connla's Well, but when it does it is carried downstream and if, passing from current to current, it is brought to your feet and you eat it, then though in no way altered, sight in you will be pure wonder. Then, seeing ordinary things in the ordinary way you had always seen them, sight in you will be more visionary than vision …

Q: Are you implying that such sight isn't native to us?

A: No, I am not. As Bran mac Feabhail who set out in quest of it discovered, the Otherworld is a way of perceiving this world. Quite simply, the Otherworld is silver-branch perception, and this fits in with the persistent claim that ours is a land of three immaculate dimensions, Banbha, Fódhla and Éire. And be sure of this: however ravaged and spoiled and polluted it might be by our Fomorian abuse of it, Éire in itself is still immaculate. And this isn't only true of Ireland. It is true of no matter what country. It is true of the world at large. The Bhagavad Gita, the Song of God that Manannán, god of the sea, sang to us at sea – that he could as easily sing to us in New York or in Tokyo, because reality there is as immaculate as it is here this morning in the mountains of Kerry. Banbha, Fódhla and Éire are immaculate dimensions of New York as much as they are immaculate dimensions of the furze-yellow world between me and Torc Mountain. silver-branch perception is as possible in the Ruhr Valley as it is here. There too, the corn is orient and immortal wheat.

Time, meeting Banbha on Slieve Mish, to shake their apprehensive hawk talons out of our hands.

Time, meeting Fódhla on Cnoc Gréne, to shake their apprehensive hawk talons out of our eyes.

Time, meeting Éire on Uisnech, to shake their apprehensive hawk talons out of our minds.

Q: No small matter in that case to come ashore into Ireland, no small matter to settle in Ireland?

A: We have come ashore into Ireland and we have settled here when we know that any well we dip our buckets into is Connla's Well.

Q: But who is Connla?

A: If you do not know him from within yourself as yourself, then you will never know him at all.

Q: And Ireland? Again I ask, what of Ireland?

A: My hope is that it is still a dangerous place.

Q: Meaning what?

A: My hope is that the Owenmore River, and rivers like it,

and that Torc Mountain, and mountains like it, can still subvert us back into sanity.

Q: And the stories you tell?

A: Better imagined and better told than they are here, they could be forms of our sensibility and categories of our understanding.

Better imagined and better told than they are here, they could be an alternative to Balar's evil eye, to the national nemtenga.

Better imagined and better told than they are here, they could be In Tenga Bithnua.

Better imagined and better told than they are here, they could be a way of saying

Ailiu Iath n-hErend

Q: But if to reach and settle in Ireland we have to come in not over but through nine waves, each wave a yet deeper initiation into yet deeper wonder. And if, having come through all that, we must continue into and through a swordless safari of stories, each story a challenge to further integration not just of instinct but of insight, if we must be thrown on the bonefire of all our incarnations past and to come, and if, not there yet, we must now respond to the invitations extended to us by Danu, Manannán, Cú Roí and Christ, then who will make it?

A: We are talking about realizing our highest human possibilities, and what is wrong with that? What is wrong about emerging into a sense of wonder? What is wrong about the integration of deepest instinct and highest insight? What is wrong about silver-branch perception? What is wrong about the road of ashes? What is wrong about metanoesis? What is wrong about a graduation from anthropus to deinanthropus? What is wrong about a mystical ascent between the Paps of Danu? What is wrong about the gap between those divine breasts being the ultimate gap into Ultimate Ireland? If the alternative is a republic such as we have now, what is so wrong about an Énflaith? What is so wrong about the democracy of royalty in Tara? What is so wrong about the royalty of everyone? Not institutional royalty, or royalty by coronation, but royalty that Conaire and Cormac emerged into, royalty of nature.

Oldest democracy, newest democracy, truest democracy, surest democracy, is the democracy of the Road of Initiations. From the moment the Paschal Candle is set up by my cradle to the moment it is set up by my coffin, the Christian road is a road of initiations. In the sense that everyone is welcome onto it, it is the most democratic of roads, but how vastly foolish we would be were we to set out upon it if waving a bill of human rights. Seek to inscribe no such bill on the Paschal Candle. Seek to hang no such bill from the solstice sunspear.

Q: You have said elsewhere that it is as dangerous to ask too much of ourselves as it is to ask too little of ourselves.

A: That I believe is true, but much as nature hates the vacuum so does it hate stagnation. As its ventriloquist, or as its plenipotentiary maybe, Blake has Hell say:

>The cistern contains, the fountain overflows,

also

>Expect poison from a standing water.

But Blake didn't erect a sign saying:

>BEWARE

>AS A LUNG CAN COLLAPSE SO CAN A PSYCHE

and of this be sure:

>A PSYCHOSIS IS BIGGER THAN THE UNIVERSE
>IN WHICH IT HAPPENS

Q: Suggesting to me that even if we substitute the Orphic note for the sword the safari inland that you are proposing is nonetheless reckless and should be called off.

A: An Énflaith, I believe, is safely attainable. Ultimacy, in the sense of ultimate living to ultimate purpose, that can be the choice of individuals within it. Or outside it for that matter.

Q: You have capitulated to common sense, haven't you?

A: Strange though it was, a dream I dreamed last night makes sense, makes common sense to me.

Q: Tell me.

A: I dreamed that Fál, the stone phallus at Tara, screeched its approval of us.

Q: As we are now?

A: As we once were, as we will be.

Q: To all of which, as artistic Lucifer, as artistic Light Bringer, Joyce would say, 'non serviam'.

A: Yes, but think of the theranthropic disaster that was Minoan Crete.

Q: You have lost me.

A: As the supreme artificer, Daedalus was complicit in that disaster. Instead of attempting to integrate animal instinct in us, he helped to suppress it, impounding it in the last chasm of a labyrinth under civilization. It didn't work. And Joyce knew that it didn't work, and in all his subsequent work it was to Daedalus, his chosen archetype, that he was Lucifer, it was to Daedalus he said, 'non serviam'.

So here, in this text. In this text we do not excavate a labyrinth under Tara, or, for that matter, under Eccles Street. On the contrary. It is because they have so perfectly integrated instinct in them that Conaire Mór and Cormac mac Airt are the exemplary kings that they are. Ecumenical with all that they inwardly are, they are in consequence able to be ecumenical with the world around them. In this both Minos and Pericles have much to learn from them.

Q: Puck Fair, you are saying, not the Labyrinth?

A: Solutions come more readily in mathematics than in human affairs, so I hope that what I have written here cannot be reduced to any such slogan.

Q: In that case, by your own admission, you aren't doing anything very definite here?

A: Here we are seeking to do what Joyce sought to do, not in exile, but at home. Relying on our native inheritance and abilities, we are seeking to evoke a consciousness and a conscience, in the first instance for ourselves. Happily, we can evoke both the one and the other, both being interdependent, from intuitions and aspirations already well tested. Our task is to reinstitute the Énflaith, this time not on anthropic but on deinanthropic foundations. That done, we will go back among Europeans, to educate them, in Minoan Knossos, in Periclean Athens, in imperial Rome, in Medicean Florence, in revolutionary Paris, and, yet more urgently, where Mistah Kurtz grew up, in Brussels.

Q: Columba and Columbanus all over again?

A: The Énflaith is a consciousness and a conscience we could ascend the Rhine and the Seine and the Tiber with. And the Volga and the Yangtze and the Ganges and the Congo and the Amazon and the Mississippi – all those rivers we should also ascend bringing this consciousness and this conscience with us.

Instead of a legal constitution to be interpreted for huge sums of money by lawyers let us have a constitution of stories, a genome of stories, to be interpreted for nothing by poets.

Q: A genome of stories?

A: Yes, in the literal sense of stories that will be culturally genetic to us, will generate us culturally in instinct, eye and mind.

Q: To be interpreted late at night in a pub in Knocknagree by the likes of Eoghan Ruadh Ó Suilleabháin?

A: To be lived by him and by us. In this I am thinking of Holderlin and Heidegger. They believe we can sing not sword our way ashore. They believe we can dwell poetically.

Q: But I am not so sure that you can fully trust Amhairghin Glúngheal, even though he in a sense is the archetypal poet. Him you would also throw on the bonefire of all his animal and human incarnations. And as for the knowledge he parades – you would not I believe be entirely unhappy to see it going up in smoke, such is your delight in thinking of Cú Roí mac Daire walking metanoetically south by west through Ireland?

A: Proving that what I've written is so polyphonically various it cannot be reduced to a slogan, and of that I am right glad.

Q: So where does that leave us?

A: As we have indicated, there are two ways of coming ashore into Ireland. We can do so wielding a sword or we can do so singing the Orphic note.

And as with our effort to come ashore into Ireland so with our effort to come ashore on to the Earth.

Q: Are you saying that the one effort is prototype and precedent to the second?

A: No, for the reason that it suggests cultural imperialism. Think rather, as Keats once did, of the excitement of an astronomer when a new planet swims into his ken.

Recently, the planet we live on swam into our ken, and our song seeing it, our song coming back to it, our song setting foot in it, could be a song in which we name it anew, a song of two words, of one word:

BUDDH GAIA

Q: Not a destination we foresaw setting out, is it?

A: Any journey in which you fall in with Cú Roí mac Daire and with Christ is likely to end up further along than you thought or hoped it would.

Q: The result being?

A: That we mean something surprisingly and unexpectedly new when we say

Ailiu Iath n-hErend.

Book One

IRELAND, A PROPHECY

A NOTE ON PROCEDURE

Over the years I have assembled what I sometimes think of as a Tarot Pack of myths, folktales, stories, symbols, images, and here I make deliberate not random selections from it. In this I lay myself open to the charge of self-plagiarism. This charge I seek to counter on the following grounds. Taking a particular shade of red, let us place it in two different colour contexts. First, let us place it between purple and black, then, between yellow and blue, and now we find that, modified by the different colours either side of it and modifying them in turn, it looks and it actually is different in these, its two occurrences, the one from the other. Similarly with a literary text or with a leit-motif within a literary text: to locate it in different semantic contexts is, in each case, to have it mean and do different things.

Part I

Orpheus in Ireland

Preface

LIVING as he did in high revolutionary and reactionary times, Blake wrote a book called *America, A Prophecy*, also a book called *Europe, A Prophecy*. This morning, having little faith in what I was doing, I strung some stories already to hand together and, to its very great embarrassment I'm sure, I called the result, *Ireland, A Prophecy*. Prophecy not in the sense of prediction. Prophecy, rather, as an effort to elaborate a state of mind in and from which a particular people might prosper in ways hitherto uncommon. To begin with, it is likely that such a state of mind will be found only in exceptional individuals living here and there, living now and then, with long tracts of uninspired history between the exceptional now and the exceptional then. Life in our time is uninspired. Evidence everywhere suggests that we are the new Fomorians.

This effort, such as it is, falls into two parts, Orpheus in Ireland, Manannán in Ireland.

Manannán, the god of the sea as we know him, is different in character and kind from Poseidon, the god of the sea as Greeks knew him. Likewise, the Orpheus indigenous to the Irish tradition differs in character and kind from the Orpheus indigenous to the Greek tradition.

As Greeks knew him, Orpheus was in all ways the opposite of Herakles or, as he is more commonly known, Hercules.

In his efforts to open and make the land safe for human habitation, Hercules clubbed it. In its savageries, he clubbed it, clubbed it, clubbed it. All its dragon energies he clubbed, to death. Were it not for Orpheus, it would have been a safe but unreal land that the Greeks inherited, and it would have come all too easy to succeeding generations to plough its last remaining poetry out of it. Sinking down into the music common to all things, that all things are composed of, Orpheus was symphonic, more, he was homeo-phonic, with all things as, in turn, were all things, snake and lion, with him. In this wise he was able for the world more or less as he found it. At ease with the animal in himself, animals in the world around him were at ease with him.

So which will it be? In Ireland which will it be? Orpheus and his song or Hercules and his club?

As these stories show, the Orphic option, if that is what we choose, will be a struggle. Sometimes our Fomorian instincts will prevail, making themselves horrendously visible all over the land. Sometimes the boar will turn on us, tusking us right there at the liebestod heart of our dolmen love. Sometimes, like it or not, we will find ourselves back at the hell-mouth. Some nights we will hear it, the dragon scream that quenches all of Ireland's hearth-fires. Even so, as Rilke in a sonnet to Orpheus has it, *Gesang ist Dasein*, 'song is existence', and, to be fair to him, it was in and with his song of ecumenical existence that Amhairghin Glúngheal sought to open a way for the Celts into Ireland. In this, for now, he was an Orpheus not a Hercules. For now, in his *Dasein*, he was a singer invoking the land of Ireland not a spear hungry to plunder it. For reasons to be canvassed, it didn't work, and so it is that here, in this effort, we look forward to a day in our past when, one for all, one of us came ashore singing the Sea-God's Sea Gita. In the meantime, at a depth of ourselves and of our tradition not often visited, there he is, Ogma at sea, bringing the music of Ireland home to Ireland. Always, at that depth, there is someone walking naked to Tara. At that depth, always, there is someone who is willing to be death-rattled, death-rattled, death-rattled back into our first shamanic way.

'And you, Fionn,' Oscar asked 'what music most pleases you?'

'The music of what happens,' Fionn said.

Following on from this, Fionn might some day find it in him to be sym-phonic, even homeo-phonic, with the music of what happens. This, as we have suggested, is the Orphic way. In a dimension of Ireland called Fódhla, it is the way.

Call it Fódhla, call it Iath nAnann.

Iath nAnann always is, and the day overt, official Ireland loses touch with it, on that day official Ireland, called Éire, will sicken and die, all people's eyes and minds as knotted as their navel cords, drawing no nourishment now from nature, not drawing it from anything anywhere, within or without.

Postponing that day, there he is, the one who will be Ireland's Ollamh Fódhla, walking in his people's dream of him.

In Ireland, having many simultaneous and sequent identities, and living as he does in many ages, Orpheus has many names.

In one age you will find him living in a hut by the hellmouth. In another age you will find him living in a house that is mirrored in Linn Feic, the most sacred pool of Ireland's most sacred river.

My house is mirrored in Linn Feic.

In a sense therefore I sleep in Linn Feic, I dream in Linn Feic.

At a sleeping depth of me that I'm not aware of, maybe I am a salmon in Linn Feic, and maybe I swim upstream every night, all the way up into the Otherworld, all the way up into Connla's Well. At that depth of myself, maybe the shadows of the Otherworld hazel are always upon me, are always upon all of us, letting wisdom and wonder drop down into us.

In yet another age, changed again, you will find him crossing his yard at nightfall with Ireland's oldest landscape in a bag on his back.

Wonders are spoken of you in Ireland, Orpheus.
Listening to Fintan mac Bochra we are listening to you:

As the folktale sees I see.
As the folktale lives I live.
And the path to my door, that too is a folktale.
Coming here, you either undergo what people undergo in a folktale, or you will never lift my latch.

Little wonder I so rarely hear my latch being lifted.
Little wonder I so rarely hear my latch being lifted.
Little wonder I so rarely hear my latch being lifted.

And the Prophecy, as prediction: that what has been will be again; that one day, one for all, one of us will come ashore singing Manannán's Song.

In Ireland as in Greece, Orpheus needs a music lesson.

Bringing Home Our Stolen Soul

IN THE MYTHIC imagination of Indo-Europeans it is the great battle. In India it is the battle between the Devas and the Asuras. In Greece it is the battle between the Gods and the Giants. In Nordic countries it is the battle between the Aesir and the Vanir. In Ireland it is the battle between the Tuatha Dé Danann and the Fomorians.

An old book says this about the Tuatha Dé Danann:

Bátar Tuatha Dé Danann i n-indsib túascertachaib an domuin, aig foglaim fesa ocus fithnasachta ocus druidechtai ocus amaidechtai ocus amainsechta, combtar fortilde for súthib cerd ngenntlichtae.

Living as they then were in the northern islands of the world, the Tuatha Dé Danann spent their time acquiring visionary insight and foresight and hindsight, acquiring the occult knowledge and the occult arts of the wizard, the druid, the witch, these, together with all the magical arts, until, masters in everything concerning them, they had no equals in the world.

Little wonder then that it was in a great magical cloud that they came to Ireland, landing in the mountains of Conmaicne Re in Connacht. In truth they were a race of gods but, for all the occult arts at their command, it was their particular delight to be of one mind with the wind and the rain. Great warrior though he was, Ogma knew that a spear that went through him wouldn't open him out half as much to the Otherworld as the call of a curlew calling in a bog would open him out to this world. And Dien Cecht, their leech, he had the look of an upland thorn bush that has long ago yielded to the endless, night and day persuasions of the prevailing wind and is now no more than a current, than the memory of a current, in it.

In the end you could walk through the land and not know they were in it.

Their features hanging like seaweed when the tide is out, their tongues the colour and shape of cormorant's tongues, the clamour of ocean in their talk, Fomorians came ashore.

Forests cut down, rivers re-routed, towers everywhere, it was soon clear that it must come to a fight.

It did. In Magh Tuired.

Never before or since did the Battle Hag screech as she screeched that night, her mouth bleeding in excited anticipation of the greatest battle that would ever be fought in Ireland. So long and loud and piercing was her third screech, it cut gaps in the mountains, it sent the incoming tides back out and as far away as west Munster where a man was talking that night to his wife he didn't finish what he had to say because, sliced down the middle, the two halves of him and of what he was saying fell either side of her.

It was that kind of battle.

As much because of what their wizards did as what their warriors did, victory was with the Tuatha Dé Danann, or so it seemed.

When the outcome was still in doubt Mathgen, their chief wizard, went chanting forward and so burning a thirst did he cause not just the mouths but in the minds of the fighting Fomorian warriors that, whatever the cost, victory or defeat not counting now, they must find water, but find it they didn't because, changing his chant, Mathgen dried up the rivers and streams and lakes and wells of Ireland and there they were, deliriously crossing bogs and climbing mountains, the sound of far away, illusory waterfalls calling them out over precipices to their death.

What the Tuatha Dé Danann didn't yet know was that the chief wizard of the Fomorians could make himself invisible and it was he, altogether more clever than Mathgen, who single-handedly turned what they had already begun to think of as their greatest victory into their greatest defeat, and this he did by going right to the heart of Tuatha Dé Danann country, into a fortress there, and stealing their great harp called Harmonizes Us to All Things.

Next day at the very beginning of their victory celebrations, the Tuatha Dé discovered and suffered their loss.

Putting it to his lips, the chief piper could find no music in his pipe.

Putting it to his lips, the chief trumpeter could find no music in his trumpet.

Putting his bow to it, the chief fiddler could find no music in his fiddle.

Tapping it with his drumstick, the chief drummer could find neither rhythm nor music in his drum.

Opening her mouth, the chief singer could find no music in her voice.

And the curlew didn't call in the bog.

And the blackbird in the willows didn't sing.

Asleep that night on the nine hazel wattles of vision, Mathgen saw what had happened. Macguarch, the chief of Fomorian wizards, had stolen the harp and in stealing that he had stolen the music of Ireland.

That very day, their tongues the colour and shape of cormorant's tongues, the Tuatha Dé were the new Fomorians.

Only Ogma, he being who he was, didn't capitulate to the country-wide epidemic of forgetfulness and brutishness.

Curious about him in the old days, Coirpre the poet had put it to him. 'Which is it?' he asked. 'Is it integrity of being or integrity of decision and principle that makes you the kind of man that you are?'

'Nothing so frail as either,' Ogma replied.

'Then what is it?' Coirpre asked.

'There is something more to me than my life,' Ogma said.

'And that something more?' Coirpre asked. 'What is it? Is it in mountains and stars?'

'Without it there would be no mountains and stars,' Ogma replied.

'So, your life deriving from it, would it also without anguish enable you to surrender your life, to lay down your life?'

'It is only when you surrender your life that you most plentifully derive your life from it,' Ogma answered.

And that's how it happened. From the day that Coirpre took serious notice of him as a man apart, Ogma was the first and the only philosophical question that bothered and intrigued the Tuatha Dé Danann.

On the third morning after the theft, Ogma walked west through the songless land, all the way west to the coast. Finding a rowing boat that was big enough to be a sail boat, he put to sea. He came to the towered land. Telling no one his business, just being the man he was, a man apart, he walked, no one daring to challenge him, through all outer and inner defences. Armed doorkeepers making way for him, he entered the fortress at the heart of the country, he took the harp and, as with everyone's permission, he walked back to the shore and, its stolen music coming with him, he came home to Ireland.

Now it was the turn of the Fomorians. Now for the first time in their history they were philosophically bothered. More intrigued than bothered.

In the end, after much concentrated, deep thinking, a thing they weren't used to, they concluded that it was a fair exchange, the harp for the question. It wasn't a question they had to ask. All they had to do was close their eyes and they would see it walking among them.

'How did you do it?' Coirpre asked. 'How without lifting a sword did you bring the music of Ireland back to Ireland? If you hadn't brought it back, I wouldn't be asking you this question because mine would be a cormorant's mind, mine would be a cormorant's tongue, and you I'd think of as a man like all others, like myself.'

'As we discovered too late,' Ogma said, 'it was by being able to be invisible that Macguarch stole our music. It was by being able to be visible, all the way out from the ground of my being and their being, that I was able to walk past them bringing it home. Also, I didn't project any obstacles out of myself. I didn't project those monsters and dragons that so often contest the hero's way. There is no part of my mind that I'm not at ease with, that isn't at ease with me.'

So it was that, after all their wars, Fomorians and Tuatha Dé were united by a common question, Ogma.

And now again, harmonized to all things, the Tuatha Dé were of one mind with the wind and the rain. Now again, you could walk through the land and not know they are in it. Yet we, a rougher people who came later to Ireland, out alone in lonely places we will sometimes hear their music. Airs we have heard and, merging our souls with them, we have put out own words to them, calling them 'The Cuilfhionn', 'Caisheal Mumhan', 'Slán Le Maigh', 'Port Na bPucaí', 'Eibhlín a Rún', 'Róisín Dubh' and 'Danny Boy'.

It is why our tongues aren't cormorant tongues. It is why, whatever our history, we can still hear a curlew calling in a bog.

Tailtiu Revisited

AMHAIRGHIN Glúngheal their shape-shifting poet standing as stag, as hawk, as boar, as spear, in the prow, it was in what looked like a fleet of initiations not ships that the Celts sailed up Kenmare Bay into Ireland. Setting his right foot on land, Amhairghin sang:

Am gaeth i mmuir
Am tond trethan
Am fuaim mara
Am dam secht ndrenn
Am séig i n-aill
Am dér gréne
Am cáin
Am torc ar gail
Am hé i llind
Am loch i mmaig
Am brí dánae
Am gaí i fodb feras fechtu
Am dé delbas do chind codnu

Cóich é nod gleith clochor slébe?
Cia ón cotagair aesa éscai?
Cia dú i llaig funiud gréne?
Cia bier buar ó thigh Temrach?

Cia buar Tethrach tibde?
Cia dain, cia dé, delbas faebru?
Andind; ailsiu cáinte im gaí, cáinte gaithe.

I am a wind in the sea
I am a sea-wave upon the land
I am the roar of ocean
I am a stag of seven fights
I am a hawk on a cliff
I am a tear-drop of the sun
I am fair
I am a boar for valour
I am a salmon in a pool
I am a lake in a plain
I am the excellence of arts
I am a spear waging war with plunder
I am a god who forms subjects for a ruler

Who can explain the stone designs of the mountain?
Who invokes the ages of the moon?
Where lies the setting of the sun?
Who droves the cattle from the stalls of Tetra?
The jocund cattle of Tetra, who or what are they?
What man, what god, forges the sun-spear, forges the
    sword of light?
Then, indeed, I invoked a satirist ... a satirist of wind.

Still liminal to sea and land, a neither this nor that between
hawk and human, he sings, his intention to name things in their
plentifulness, to show himself willing to flourish with the flour-
ishing world:

Iascach muir
Mothach tir
Tomaidm n-eisc
Iasca and
Fo thuind en
Lethach mil
Partach lag

Tomaidm n-eisc
Iascach muir

Fish-abounding sea
Fruitful land
Irruption of fish
Fishing there
Bird under wave
Great sea-dragon
Crab burrow
Irruption of fish
Fish-abounding sea

Liminality lived, the Celts flourished inward into Ireland. High on Slieve Mish mountain they met the goddess of Irish sovereignty, she presenting herself as Banbha. 'What you are doing is not to my liking,' she said, 'but if it must be, then I ask that you will call the land by my name, I ask that you will call it Banbha.'

Amhairghin agreed, and he and his people moved on. Farther inland, on Cnoc Áine, there she was again, the goddess of Irish sovereignty, appearing to them this time as Fódhla. 'What you are doing is not to my liking,' she said, 'but if it must be, then I ask that you will call the land by my name, I ask that you call it Fódhla.'

Amghairghin agreed and he and his people moved on. On the Hill of Uisnech, at the heart of the country, it was as Éire that the goddess of Irish sovereignty showed herself to them. Acceding to her request, Amhairghin said, 'Yes, we will call the land by your name, we will call it Éire.'

Continuing, the Celts came to Tara and waiting for them there were three kings, MacCuill the king of the dimension of Ireland called Banbha, MacCecht the king of the dimension of Ireland called Fódhla, and MacGrene, the king of the dimension of Ireland called Éire.

'Had we known you were coming,' MacCuill said, 'we'd have gone south to challenge you.'

Seeing justice in their case, Amghairghin decided that he and his people would return to their ships and, boarding them, would bring them round and go back out over nine waves.

Out over nine waves, in each wave an awakening to wonder, they sailed, and then the storm struck, scattering the ships. Suspecting that it was a magically conjured storm, Amhairghin asked a boy to climb the mast and yes, it wasn't blowing above the sails, so this was it, the resident people, if people they were, fighting not for the first time for their world. A wonder-worker himself, Amhairghin took them on. Sure of the calling, conjuring power in his words, he invoked the land of Ireland:

> *Ailiu iath n-hErend*
> *Hermach hermach muir*
> *Mothach mothach sliab*
> *Srathach srathach caill*
> *Cithach cithach aub*
> *Essach essach loch*

> I invoke the land of Ireland
> Shining shining sea
> Fertile fertile mountain
> Flourishing flourishing wood
> Plentiful plentiful river
> Fish-rich, fish-rich lake

It worked. Ireland and everything in it, all its mountains, animals, woods, rivers and lakes, came over on to his side. Also, as though the magic power that sustained it had suddenly failed, the storm ceased. The dispersed ships, if that is what they were, reconvened as a fleet off the mouth of the Boyne. Wind and tide favouring, the Celts made landfall a long ways upriver. Next day, at Tailtiu, victory was with them. Sadly ever afterwards for Ireland, all that was divine in the land retreated to the grave-mounds and to the lonely places.

AFTERTHOUGHTS

I stand before Labby Rock in Sligo and before Newgrange on the Boyne and I find myself thinking that the coming of the Celts to Ireland was a cultural disaster. A worse disaster, culturally, than the coming of the Vikings, than the coming of Cromwell and his religious roundheads.

What, compared with Newgrange, is Navan Fort? What, compared with Labby Rock, is the Táin Bó Cuailgne?

In the sense that it means defeat for a more sanctifying way of knowing and being in the world, Tailtiu is an infinitely sadder word than Kinsale.

By what name did its builders know Newgrange? By what names did they know the sun, the moon, the Boyne itself? What was their word for death? In every word and work of it, was their language as hospitable to reality as Newgrange itself is hospitable to the winter-solstice sun? Was their language so open to reality that it could travel down into the roots of its seeing and knowing, illuminating its seeing, illuminating its knowing? We do not know. Tailtiu was defeat for the language of the megalith builders. It was defeat, that is, for a way of seeing and knowing the world. How grand a way it was we see when we look at

Labby Rock

As well as being saddened by what was done to them, Celts should be saddened by what they themselves did.

In Ireland, Celts destroyed a greatness they themselves never attained to.

Bíodh brón ort, a Róisín
Lament your victory at Tailtiu

How trustworthy is Amhairghin's Song of Himself? Since it is the song of his superior claim to Ireland we should at the very least continue wide awake and critically alert listening to it. We have of course heard the like before, from Krishna, an avatar of the great god Vishnu. Here, as his charioteer, he talks to Arjuna, a great warrior, before the Battle of Kuruktshetra:

I am the Self established
In the heart of all contingent beings;
Also, I am the beginning, middle and end
Of all contingent beings.

Among the Adityas Vishnu I am,
Among lights the radiant sun,
Among the Maruts Maricí I am,
Among stars I am the moon.

Of the Vedas the Sama Veda I am
Indra among the gods;
Among the senses I am mind,
Among contingent beings thought.

Among the Rudras Shiva I am,
Among sprites and monsters Kuvera.
Of the Vasus I am Fire,
Among the mountains I am Meru.

Of household priests know that I
Am the chief, Brihaspati.
Among warlords I am Skanda,
Among lakes I am the ocean.

Bhrigu I am among the mighty seers,
Among utterances Om.
Among sacrifices I am the sacrifice of muttered prayer,
Among things immovable the Himalayas.

Among all trees the holy fig tree,
Narada among the celestial seers;
Citraratha among the heavenly minstrels,
Among perfected beings Kapila, the silent sage.

Among horses know that I
Am Uccaihsravas, from nectar born,
Among princely elephants Airavata:
Among men I am the King.

Of weapons I am the thunderbolt,
Among cows the milch cow of desires;

I am Kandarpa, generating seed,
Among serpents I am Vasuki.

Of Naga-serpents Ananta I am,
Of water-dwellers, Varuna.
Of the ancestors I am Aryaman,
Among those who subdue I am Yama.

Among demons Prahlada I am,
Among those who reckon Time;
Among beasts I am the lion,
Among birds Garuda.

Among those who purify I am Wind,
Rama I am among men-at-arms,
Among water-monsters I am the crocodile,
Among rivers I am the Ganges ...

Listening to Krishna we are sure the 'I' of his many 'I ams' is the innermost Self, is atman Brahman, the Divine Ground of all being. Listening to Amhairghin we cannot be sure that the 'I' of his 'I ams' isn't ego, and if it is then we are dealing with the serious insanity of ego-inflation.

But even if we give him the benefit of the doubt, what we might ask is the value in adding the experience of being a stag, a hawk, a salmon, a boar, to the experience of being human? What is the value in adding the experience of being a plunder-hungry spear to the experience of being human? What is the value of adding the experience of being wind and wave to the experience of being human? The truth is such additions add nothing to us. To be human, it has been justly said, is to be a microcosm, it is to be the universe in little. The elemental energies of wind and wave and the animal energies of stag and boar are native to us therefore. Jacob Boehme puts neither a stag's nor a boar's tooth in it:

In man is all whatsoever the sun shines upon or heaven contains, also hell and all the deeps.

And it was, as it were, on a Mesozoic shore of his own mind that Nietzsche set his not so foreign foot:

I have discovered for myself that the old human and animal life, indeed the entire prehistory and past of all sentient being, works on, loves on, hates on, thinks on, in me.

When it comes down to it, Amhairghin Glúngheal, the poet who was prow to the Celtic invasion of Ireland, is claiming nothing particularly more than our common phylogenetic inheritance. The difference between him and Nietzsche is that while he parades it Nietzsche is perturbed by it. Given what it is we are talking about, surely the perturbation is safer than the parade.

We are after all talking about something as serious as our emergence into Ireland. So the question is: with what vision of ourselves and our world do we sail up Kenmare Bay? With what vision of ourselves and our world do we set foot on that shingle shore?

What is clear is this: now in our day we need someone who has the gifts and the ability and the willingness to be Amhairghin Glúngheal to a new emergence, to a new anodos, into Ireland; we need someone who, having gone back out over nine waves, re-emerges singing the new song among us.

The truth is this: those nine waves that surround Ireland and its islands are nine initiations into nine wholly unexpected dimensions of reality. To properly come ashore into Ireland therefore we need to sail, not over them, but into them and through them. Taking them at face value, the Celts sailed in over them. Hence the sadness of their subsequent history here.

True of Celts, true of Christians, true of Vikings, true of Anglo-Normans.

True of the English who came.

In over the waves they all came.

Also, who now walks out of the common dimension of Ireland called Éire and sets up house by a river in Fódhla, its more mystical dimension? Since when has a great teacher and legislator come back among us out of Fódhla? Since when, passing him on the road, have we said, that is him, among us in our day he is

Ollamh Fódhla

Ireland without an Amghairghin, a poet who with his song opens a way into Ireland for us.

Ireland without an Ollamh Fódhla, a sage who comes back speaking Upanishads among us.

Having failed to come poetically ashore into Ireland the Celt has failed in Ireland.

Bíodh brón ort, a Róisín

And yet, a doubt remains. And so, having recourse to a possibly creative misreading, can we not think that, in singing his Song of Himself, Amhairghin is as it were carving a totem pole of who we elementally and phylogenetically are, indeed of who we microcosmically are, right there before our eyes?

Singing it with him we are carving it with him:

Am gaeth i mmuir
Am tond trethan
Am fuaim mara
Am dam secht ndrenn …

Ireland's first totem pole set up where it was first sung, and where it has now been carved, at the head of Kenmare Bay.

Catching sight of it as we come in from the sea, it puts it to us that to come ashore into Ireland is to come ashore into ourselves.

Reaching Uisnech, what better can we do than to give the benefit of the doubt, if not yet to the singer, then to the song, and this we can do by proclaiming a constitution that acknowledges the One in the Many, that the philosophical justification for enfranchising all things, equally, a bush having equal rights with a bear, a calf or a dropped fawn having equal rights with a child.

Soon in Ireland

The Birdreign

Ailiu Iath n-hErend.

Fintan mac Bochra

THE GEOGRAPHY of my mind is the geography of the world I walk in. In the geography of my mind and, there-fore, also in the geography of the world I walk in, are Sidh ar Feimhin, Linn Feic, Dá Chích na Morrígna and Connla's Well. And if you ask me about life, about what we haven't eyes for in this life, I will talk to you about Dá Chích na Morrígna and the paths to Sidh ar Feimhin. And the stars, if you ask me about the stars I will tell you that only they who have seen them mirrored in Linn Feic have knowledge of them, only they who have seen them mirrored in that divine deep within themselves can call themselves astronomers. And Connla's Well, at Connla's Other-world Well it was I first realized that being human is a habit. It can be broken. Like the habit of going down to the river by this path rather than that, I broke it. And so it is that, although I always know who I am, I can never be sure that what I am going to sleep at night is what I will be when I wake up in the morn-ing. In me the shape-shifts of sleep survive into waking. What I'm saying is, my shape depends on my mood. In one mood, as you can see, I'm an old man, old in the way weather-lore is old, old in the way old stories are old. In another mood I'm a salmon in Lough Derg. In a mood that lasted from the coming of Partholon to the coming of the Milesians I was a hawk in Achill.

Yes, that's how it is. You only need to break the habit once, the habit of being human I mean, and then you will be as you were between death and rebirth. Between death and rebirth our bodies are mind-bodies, and that means they are alterable. Alterable at will. We only have to will it and it happens, we flow from being a swan in Lough Owel into being a hind on Slieve Bloom into being a hare on Beara.

If for some reason he crosses into our world, the hare will have one red ear.

That's how it is.

What's possible for all of us there is possible for some of us here.

Mostly, though, we've forgotten all this, but folktales remember. Folktales aren't afraid. On its way to the well at the world's end, a folktale will stop by a rock and tell you that every seventh year, at Samhain, it turns into an old woman driving a cow. On its way to Linn Feic, a folktale will sit with you under a bush and, where a bard might tell you the history of your people awake, that bush will tell you the much more serious history of your people asleep.

And the folktale knows what so many people no longer know. It knows how to walk the path to Connla's Well. On the way to Connla's Well the world has shaken off the habit of being worldly. On the way to Connla's Well we come to see that the world's habit of being worldly is not in the world, it is in our eyes.

As the folktale sees I see.
As the folktale lives I live.
And the path to my door, that too is folktale.
Coming here, you either undergo what people undergo in a folktale or you'll never lift my latch.

Little wonder I so rarely hear my latch being lifted.
Little wonder I so rarely hear my latch being lifted.
Little wonder I so rarely hear my latch being lifted.

Ollamh Fódhla

A S I S the case with all other rivers, our river has its source in Connla's Well. And that is why we learn to speak. For us, to learn to speak is to learn to say:

Our river has its source in the Otherworld Well.

And anything we say about the hills and anything we say about the stars is a way of saying:

A hazel grows over the Otherworld Well our river has its source in.

Our time being so other than Otherworld time, it isn't often, in our time, that a hazelnut falls into Connla's Well, but when it does it is carried downstream and if, passing from current to current, it is brought to your feet and you eat it, then though in no way altered, sight in you will be pure wonder. Then, seeing ordinary things in the ordinary way you had always seen them, sight in you will be more visionary than vision.

To know, and to continue to know, that any well we dip our buckets into is Connla's Well is why we are a people.

We are a river people.

Exile for us is to live in a house that isn't river-mirrored.

Our river isn't only a river. It is also the moon-white cow

who will sometimes walk towards us, but not all the way towards us, on one or another of its banks.

The river and the cow we call by the same name. We call them Boann.

Boann, the moon-white cow.
Boann, the gleaming river.
In dreams I know it as cow.
Awake I know it as river.

And my house isn't only river-mirrored. It is mirrored in Linn Feic, its most sacred pool. And this is so because, by difficult and resisted destiny, I am ollamh to my people. They call me Ollamh Fódhla. In their view of me, Boann, the gleaming river, has carried a hazelnut to my feet.

As these things often do, it began in sleep, in dreams in the night: standing in my door I'd be tempted to think he was only a short morning's walk away, and yet it would often be nightfall before I'd at last turn back, not having made it. A sense I had is that the man I was seeking to reach was myself as I one day would be. In the most frightening of all the dreams I dreamed at that time a man who had no face came towards me and said, 'You are worlds away from him.' When he next came towards me he had a face and he said, 'You are as far away from him as waking is from dreaming.' In the end it was my own voice, more anguished than angry, that I heard: it isn't distance, measurable in hours or days of walking, that separates you from what you would be. It is states of mind, yours more than his.

Defeated, I settled back into my old ways. At this time of year that meant that one morning I'd pull my door shut behind me and drive my cattle to the high grazing ground between the Paps of Morrigu.

My father who quoted his father had always assured me that there was no sacrilege in this. According to the oldest ancestor we had hearsay of, it was in no sense a right that we claimed. Fearfully, it was a seasonal rite we were called upon to undergo. This I took on trust, allowing that there was something more than good husbandry at stake.

Up here, summer after summer since I was a boy, we shook off the vexations and the weariness of winter enclosure.

Up here the gods were not fenced in.

Up here, when we heard him neighing, we knew that the horse god couldn't be cut down to cult size, couldn't be made to serve religious need.

Up here there is a rock. It so challenges our sane sense of things that I long ago capitulated to the embarrassment of crediting what my father and his father before him used to say about it, that every seven years, at Samhain, it turns into an old woman driving a cow.

Sensing my difficulties, my father was blunt: if in the eyes of the world you aren't embarrassed by your beliefs about the world then you may conclude that the wonder-eye that is in all of us hasn't yet opened in you.

That's how it was with me in those days. No sooner had I learned the world and learned my way in it than, standing in front of a rock or a tree, I'd have to unlearn it. I'd hear a story and think that's it, that's how the world is, that story will house me, but then there she'd be, the old woman driving her cow in through my front door and out through my back door, leaving me homeless yet again.

And it wasn't just anywhere I was homeless. I was homeless on the high grazing ground between the Paps of Morrigu, and it wasn't by hearsay that, however red-mouthed she was, Morrigu was divine, all the more divine in my eyes because, like the horse god who neighed only at night, she would never submit to religious servility. Though a people prayed to her she wouldn't send rain in a time of drought or stand in battle with them against an invader.

Worship of Morrigu, of red-mouthed Morrigu, had to be pure.

And that's what I did up here.

Up here every summer I lived between the breasts of a goddess who, in her form as skald crow, called above me everyday, circled and called, searching for afterbirths, searching for corpses, searching for carrion.

The contradiction ploughed me. It ploughed me and harrowed me. 'Twas as if the breasts of the Mother Goddess had become the Paps of the Battle Goddess. And to live between the Paps was to live in trepidation of the divine embrace.

Sometimes hearing her call as a skald crow calls I would hear a demand: you must be religious but in being religious you must have no recourse to religion.

So that is it, I thought. That is the seasonal rite. To be religious here is to fast from religion.

These were heights I wasn't continuously able for. Always by summer's end I'd have lost my nerve, and now again I would pull a door shut behind me and I would go down, me and my cattle, my cattle going down to the shelter of the woods and swards along the river, and I going down to the shelter of traditional religion and story.

Here, as well as being a moon-white cow, the goddess is Boann, the gleaming river.

Down here, we are river-mirrored. And since it is the same sacred river that mirrors us, we are a people.

My house is mirrored in Linn Feic.

In a sense therefore I sleep in Linn Feic, I dream in Linn Feic.

At a sleeping depth of me that I'm not aware of, maybe I am a salmon in Linn Feic, and maybe I swim upstream every night, all the way up into the Otherworld, all the way up into Connla's Well. At that depth of myself, maybe the shadows of the Otherworld hazel are always upon me. Are always upon all of us, letting wisdom and wonder drop down into us.

Could it be that we are safer in our depths than we are in our heights? Or could it be that we will only be safe in our heights when we already know that we are safe in our depths?

This time the old woman didn't drive her cow through the conclusion I came to. This time, bringing a six years' solitude in the Loughcrew Hills to a sudden end, it was like a stroke, it was like waking up from waking. During an endless instant, all heights and depths had disappeared, leaving only a void, or what seemed like a void.

Twenty-six years later, sitting in my house by Linn Feic, I was able to say, it is in Divine Ground behind all depths and heights that we are safe.

That summer, sitting in my reconstructed hut between the Paps, I was able to say, it is from Divine Ground behind and within them that we become able for our depths and heights.

Coming down, at a turn on the path where I was only a short morning's walk away from them, I felt I was able for the sense that people had of me. I felt I was able to be their ollamh. Opening my door, knowing that I was mirrored by the sacred river, I felt that in that depth of me that is overarched by the Otherworld hazel I had consented to be Ollamh Fódhla.

Fír Flathemon

IT IS a story soon told. Art was king in Tara, a hill from which
on a clear day he could see his entire kingdom. It was fore-
shown to him that in a battle soon to be fought in the far west
he would be killed by Lughaidh mac Con, a pretender to the
throne. On the night before the battle he lay with Achtan the
daughter of a famous druid. In time Achtan gave birth to a boy
child. Calling him Cormac mac Airt, the druid his grandfather
chanted five protective circles about him, against wounding,
drowning, fire, sorcery and wolves. Knowing that Lughaidh
intended their destruction, Achtan sought refuge for herself and
Cormac in a trackless wilderness. As they slept together one
night on a bed of leaves a milch wolf came and stole the child.
Taking him to her cave in Keshcorran, she suckled him, he
drinking her two middle tits as dry as her five cubs drank theirs
dry.

Months later a hunter climbed towards the Keshcorran
caves. He saw the child playing with the wolves. Guessing who
he was, he waited till the whole pack had gone off on the hunt
and then he rescued him, taking him to Achtan.

Knowing how soon Lughaidh would be on the prowl,
Achtan decided to seek refuge with Fiachna Casán in Ulster.
Fiachna was Art's foster father. As she crossed a mountain at
night the wolves of Ireland came from far and near seeking the

46

child, claiming him as theirs. Surrounding them, a herd of wild horses escorted mother and child all the way to safety in Fiachna's house.

One day, a young man now, Cormac set out for Tara. Keeping the hill to his right, he came upon a woman in dishevelled distress. Enquiring the cause, she told him that her sheep had grazed the queen's woad field in the night and now they were forfeit to her.

'A shearing for a shearing, the wool for the woad, that would have been more just,' Cormac said.

Within hours the judgment was famous, known by everyone, except the king, in Tara.

When he did hear of it, Lughaidh knew that the one who delivered it was the rightful heir to the throne. Defeated in a way that he couldn't be in battle, he resigned and soon preparations were underway for Cormac's inauguration.

No small matter this. Not something for one morning only.

First, in a manner most sacred, he must marry Meadhbh, the goddess of sovereignty. Meadhbh was dangerous and strange. Could be, you would look at her and she would be the ugliest and foulest thing you could imagine. Turning away in utter, sickening revulsion you would for some reason be tempted to look back and now she would be fair beyond anything you could imagine. The one who was destined to be king must be able to lie with her foul and fair.

There was a king's chariot at Tara. Yoked to it were two horses of the same colour, horses that had never been harnessed. Wilder than the wildest horse, the chariot would rear up and throw off someone who wasn't true enough and just enough and wise enough to be king.

There were at Tara two thunderous standing stones called Blocc and Bluigne, with only a hand's breadth between them. They too must accept the one who would be king, opening before his chariot horses, letting him ride regally through.

There is in Tara a standing, stone phallus called Fál. The one who would be king must ride past it and if, as he does so, it doesn't screech against his chariot axle, he is rejected.

Cormac lay with Meadhbh, the goddess of sovereignty, fair and foul.

Stepping up into it, the royal chariot didn't rear up and throw him off.

The purple mantle on the prow of the chariot fitted him perfectly.

The two thunderous standing stones, Blocc and Bluigne, opened before his chariot horses, letting him ride regally through.

Riding past it, Fál, the stone phallus, screeched against his chariot axle.

On the morrow, Cormac, who had been suckled by a wolf, was crowned king.

Never before or since was there a reign like it in Ireland. More than swineherds could dream of or imagine there was beech mast and acorns in the woods. Salmon and sea trout ran in the rivers. Cattle were as lovely to look at in March as they were coming down from high grazing ground in October. The calls of grouse calling in the mountains were as bright as their combs. No warrior came home with the heads of his enemies hanging from the manes of his chariot horses. No druid chanted a killing or a maddening incantation. People died as they lived, at ease with a world they had flourished in. And all of this because of Fír Flathemon, the wisdom and truth and justice of the ruler.

That, in little, is the story.

Before anything else, perhaps, what we notice is how etymologically clamant it is. Art means Bear. Lughaidh mac Con means Lughaidh son of Wolf. And Cormac mac Airt means Cormac son of Bear. What we have therefore is dynastic interruption and restoration, Wolf defeating Bear in battle and Bear defeating Wolf in wisdom. Wisdom specifically in the determination and exercise of justice.

Only it isn't so exogamously simple. Between the usurpation and the restoration Wolf suckles the child who is Boy and Bear, gives her life-milk to the child who is Boy and Bear, and so it is that, in this stolen child, Boy and Bear and Wolf are foster brothers.

In the unalarmed language of legend, Cormac who is the son of a human father and mother is also a son of Bear and a son of Wolf. In a world that is still able for such things, Cormac mac Airt is Cormac mac Con in flight from Lughaidh mac Con. The child who is Boy and Bear and Wolf in flight from Wolf.

Etymologically, at this point, the story seems to be saying that at birth we are a multiplicity of shape-shifting possibilities, not an essentially unalterable unity.

In identification with Cormac, we ask who are we, and the answer is troubling.

And now a night like no other, ever, in Ireland – the wolves of Ireland, all of them, no matter where, throw back their heads and howl unanimously, and then, coming in long, lonesome strides, they surround the fleeing mother and child, claiming him as Wolf Son, their son.

The question now is: fenced ever more narrowly in by it, can we emerge from nature into culture? Can we emerge from wolfish ways into what we fondly think of as human, humane ways?

Extraordinarily, it is with the help of a herd of wild horses that we do so. Breaking through the snarling claim of nature to us, they walk with us to Fiachna's door, he a renowned druid and teacher.

How did Cormac take to culture?

Did he wolfishly reject it?

When being wolfish wasn't enough in getting his own way, would he suddenly turn bearish?

Even when he began to be more human than animal would the wolf in him suddenly steal him back into his wolfish were-wolfish ways, would the bear in him suddenly steal him back into his bearish, berserk ways?

In emotion and mood was he subject to sudden and spontaneous shapeshift?

Was it, at best, that a thin crust of human ways came to overlay his deeper and more abiding wolfish ways?

Or, all teaching and talk having failed, did he one day come thunderstruck down from the hills, wild nature and druidic culture singing a perfectly single song in him?

Noticing it, did neighbours come round to the difficult idea that the lightning had a hand in his reconstruction, in his refinement?

Finally, did they come round to the yet more difficult idea that deep within him, explaining his brightness, a diamond had formed?

Could he, in the light of that diamond, see into all worlds, into all causes of all things?

We do not know.

Having the silences and imaginative omissions of a folktale or a ballad, the story only tells us that, coming to him one morning, Fiachna said, 'Today is a good day to go south and assume kingship in Tara.'

Etymologically self-assured, he did go south.

And now again, Blocc and Bluigne opened before us.

Now again, announcing Fír Flathemon in Ireland, Fál, the stone phallus, screeched.

AFTERTHOUGHTS

Carry the lad that's born to be king over lands and lakes, over bogs and through woods, to fosterage with a druid in Ulster.

The lad who has a milch wolf for a foster mother and a druid for a foster father.

The lad who undergoes fosterage in nature before he undergoes fosterage in culture, in druidic culture.

The lad who must ever afterwards know the equal claims upon him of nature and of culture.

The lad who in virtue of natural descent from his natural father is Cormac mac Airt, is Cormac son of Bear, and who in virtue of fosterage to a wolf-mother is Cormac mac Con, is Cormac son of Wolf.

This lad who was born to be king and who became king,

did he, in heraldry flying from standard and pole and rampart-wall, declare himself to be a march-man, a man of the marches, of the march-lands, between animal and human?

Given his lineage natural and cultural, how secure in any particular identity could Cormac be? In his deepest, unremembered dreams, did he migrate among identities? Awake, would he sometimes be seized by dread of turning into a bear, by dread of turning into a wolf, by dread of becoming a were-bear, a were-wolf?

Did Cormac fear battle, thinking that in charge after charge, and blow by blow, a blind fury would build in him, and he would become a berserker?

Insecure in his identity, did Cormac ever dream that his purple, royal robe had become a bear-sack, a bear-shirt, a bear-coat? The bear-shirt, the bear-coat of a berserk?

In older times, when someone wished to become a were-wolf, he would anoint his whole body in magical oils and he would wear a girdle made of wolf-skin. Did Cormac ever dream that his wolf-mother came to him with such a girdle? To meet her on her terms was he tempted to turn wolf, to become were-wolf?

The story of this lad who is born to be king builds to a supreme crisis when, claiming him for nature, the wolves of Ireland close in on him, close in on a fugitive mother and child. Intermediaries between nature and culture, their kind co-operating in culture with humanity, a herd of wild horses break through the wolf-circle, the wolf-girdle, and escort both mother and child back into culture. Does this mean that, claimed by culture, he is now lost to nature?

Or, fostered by both, did Cormac emerge as a perfect unanimity of nature and culture in a single, supremely assured, sovereign identity, a king before he was king by copulation with Meadhbh, the goddess of sovereignty.

And this perfect unanimity of wild nature and druidic culture in him – that, surely, was the source of Fír Flathemon in him.

Wolf's milk, the milk of wild nature, that and the nurtur-
ing graces of druidic incantation and ritual gave to Cormac a
distinction at once natural and cultured, at once animal and
heraldic.

Recognizing the perfect unanimity of wild nature and
druidic culture in Cormac mac Airt, in Cormac mac Con, the
newly yoked horses at Tara didn't leap at him, Blocc and Bluigne
opened before him and, as he rode past it, Fál, the stone phallus, screeched against his chariot axle.

Heard throughout the land, it was the screech of fertility in
nature and culture.

Énflaith: The Birdreign of the Once and Future King

I

OTHER BOYS had an ancestry, I had a pedigree, and my pedigree meant it was mostly through dreaming that I would know and deal with reality. Overflowing all inner and outer banks, dreaming would sometimes be an inundation, an outcrop of waking nowhere in sight.

Even when he was near me, talking to me, my father was far away. In birdform, among birds, their underwings raucously red, is how I remember him.

Meass Buachalla was my mother. She looked after a king's cattle. She had cures. And she crossed into Otherworlds as easily as someone who has slept all night crosses into waking. Sometimes a long sojourn in an Otherworld would fall between the two parts of a conversation I'd have with her.

The birds my father flocked with could, on occasion, be murmuringly savage. Mostly, though, they were as shy as geese. Only once did I ever come close to them. Which was my father I couldn't say. When they took flight, I saw again that underwing and underweb they were raucously red.

One evening, shortly before I'd have closed it, a hurt bird, a skald crow, flew through my door. Without thinking, I held out my hand, palm downwards. She perched on it. She looked at me. She squawked three times. Then she flew back out, leaving her hurt behind. I knew I would carry that hurt for the rest of my life. And I also knew that I wouldn't be a warrior, even though that's why I had been fostered out so young to my uncle, a wide man, a man of war, and famous, his hospitality talked of from sea to sea.

After seven years I had only my hurt to go home with.

And I didn't reach home.

The path I had taken was taking me nowhere. Mountains I had in mind, it hadn't in mind. 'Twas as if it were walked only by beings who had no knowledge or need of elsewhere. Are there such beings? I wondered. I was beginning to be frightened. Are there beings for whom all elsewheres are where we are? What kind of mind have they? What kind of eyes?

At the end of three vexed days, the sunset vexed and very red, I gave up. I sat on a rock. It was strange. These thoughts I was thinking didn't seem to be my thoughts. But whose thoughts were they? Were they the land's thoughts? It was an old, old land, older than human intentions and purposes. Human intentions and purposes were nowhere visible in it. Was it taking me over? Was it thinking through me?

Could it be, I thought, that I have walked into a mood of mind or a mood of nature in which there are no intentions? Could it be, I thought, that having intentions fences me in?

But thoughts like these couldn't be my thoughts.

Thoughts like these didn't fit my forehead. They didn't fit seed or sense in me. I was afraid. Had I walked into someone's dream of me?

I got up and walked on, looking for evidence of the everyday world.

It was everywhere in evidence.

Off the path, on a patch of wet grass, was a pair of snails. Copulating they were, their horns, all eight of them, withdrawn from the distractions of a world now not necessary.

In the lee of a shag of bushes, mostly blackthorn, not yet

blossoming, was a ram.

Lying there, his head high, he was chewing the cud and between his horns, leaning forward, a magpie was picking wool for her nest.

As I approached it, noisily, a stick breaking under my feet, a pair of mallard broke in a frightened confusion of forms from a cove of reeds and then, assuming distinct duck shapes, they turned south and the water drops that fell from them left trails of expanding circles on the candour of the lake.

Three days became four days,
Three nights became four nights.

After nine days and nights I knew that, disarmed as I was, I had met my destiny. The candour of the lake in front of me, that was it.

It was a temptation to something more dangerous than sanctity.

Leaving her hurt in me, the hurt bird had disarmed me of shield and spear and sword. Had disarmed me of high horsemanship, of a right, already won, to a high place at the warrior's table.

But now the lake was disarming me, not of accoutrements and acquirements, but of something I was. And nine years later, having lived since then in a restored crannog, a high island to the north of me, patches of reeds east of me, nine years later it would still, at odd moments, disarm me of all I self seekingly was.

I would see how unworldly the world was.

There were mornings, calm and clear, when the candour of the lake was candour of hand and eye in me.

The candour of its seeing would sometimes be my seeing, seeing the mountains without distortion.

The distortion of greed.
The distortion of anger.
The distortion of love.
The distortion of hope.
The distortion of despair.

The distortion above all of intention and purpose.

At night, delight was the light in my lamp, it was the light in me. And moths came. A moth from Brí Leith.

It was her joy to find someone with whom she could be human. It was her joy to find someone who was able for the splendours of her needs at night. It was hurt in me that enabled me. We pitied the shining stars. But we knew, looking at them, that their night would come. It had come for us. All summer long all elsewheres were where we were. Tír Tairngrí was in her hair. Magh Meall was in my eyes. We walked, whenever we walked abroad, in Emain Abhlach.

II

I dreamed: my house was my grave mound. I was desolate, groping carved walls in the darkness. I found the passage. I was walking, I hoped, towards dawn. A solstice spear, a sun-spear, speared me, tumbling me back on to the sepulchral floor.

I sat with the bones of my incarnations.

I ate the food of the dead. Bird food, boar food, horse food. Someone was there.

He was gathering the bones. Bones of the bird I was, of the boar I was, of the horse I was. Of creatures unknown that I was.

He heaped them together, boar bones at the bottom, bird bones on top.

'Your bonefire,' he said, setting fire to them.

He threw me into the flames.

I was sitting in ashes when I revived.

My first breath was a last plume of smoke.

'Eat it,' he said.

As I ate the ashes, I had visions. I was walking with animals. I was kind of their kind. I was mind of their mind. I woke up. I got up. Crossing the causeway I was when I realized I had the sun-spear in my hand. It would, I realized, be in my hand whenever I needed it.

III

In a wood a voice called out.

You are now a people's dream of you. Walk in it.

Again, after a long while, it called,

Walk in it.

Six mornings later before sunrise it called,

Walk in the people's dream of you.

The last time it called the voice was an echo:

Naked, it said, naked naked naked.

Naked, like a child not ashamed, I walked out of the wood. Ahead of me, on the rough sward, grazing it, were the birds my father flocked with.

I walked towards them. They took to flight alighting not far away. I kept walking. Again they took flight, and again they alighted. And so it continued till they came to the sea. There the one who was my father turned and, assuming human form, he came to me saying, 'Walk on as you are. Walk northwards naked to Tara. You will be king.'

IV

He could escape into other species, she could escape into other worlds. I couldn't. Or rather I decided that even if I could I wouldn't. Smoke of a bonefire in my nostrils, Magh Meall long gone from my eyes, I would be loyal to the hurt human, the hurt bird. My reign would be a Birdreign.

Walking northwards naked to Tara, a sun-spear, spear of initiations, in my hand, that was my people's dream of me. That was Étain's dream of me. Throughout all my reign Étain was human. Étain was happy.

And Manannán mac Lir, he was happy one night to find Ireland, not Tír Tairngrí, in Fand's hair.

AFTERTHOUGHTS

Cometh the hour, cometh Conaire Mór, a man willing to walk in Nature's dream of him, in his people's dream of him. Reaching Tara, the savagely insurgent chariot accepted him, the royal mantle fitted him, Blocc and Bluigne, the druidic standing stones, opened before him, and, riding past it, Fál the stone phallus screeched against his chariot axle. Also, in a seriously sacred rite called the Bainis Rí, he married Meadhbh the goddess of sovereignty.

Unlike Christ, Conaire doesn't take the hurt of the world upon himself but, the exceptional hurt the skald crow left him with, that he accepts.

As tall and as wide as himself, that hurt, that wound, is the opening through which he walks out into an exceptional destiny. In accepting the wound he accepted the destiny.

Lakes unruffled by legend, the two lakes in Glendalough and Lough Derravaragh, these lakes Conaire matched in candour, and in this, ever before he was king, he was royal.

Unlike the Fisher King, it is creatively that Conaire is maimed and so it is that he can lie with a woman in the splendours of their needs, his needs and her needs, at night.

It is only in killing him regeneratively with it that the Sun, itself regenerated now at the winter solstice, can give the sun-spear to Conaire.

Having been killed regeneratively by it, Conaire can launch the sun-spear in the knowledge, sure and serene, that he will not be contaminated by the Evil that he must oppose.

Walking north to what is royal in himself, Conaire's road

becomes the Road of Ashes. The ashes of all his incarnations, past, present and to come.

For now he walks naked. Naked of accoutrements, naked of kind.

Individual and particular though he is, Conaire walking naked to Tara is all of us walking naked to Tara. Conaire walking naked to what is royal in himself is all of us walking naked to what is royal in ourselves.

In inhaling a last wisp of smoke rising from the bonefire of his incarnations, Conaire is showing himself able to acknowledge and inherit all that he has been, is showing himself able not only to coexist but to coincide with his shadow.

Having integrated it as perfectly as he has, Conaire's shadow isn't for projecting onto things. To Conaire, things are things not masks of his repressions.

It is what Conaire as king represents, the democracy of being regeneratively speared, the democracy of being reduced to ashes in the bonefire, the democracy of walking north to what is royal in us, the democracy of being right royal.

And yes, it delights Étain to be human, to have it in her to experience the limitless geographies of love and the all too unplentiful pit of despair.

Having suffered so many shapeshifts, having lived so variously, as fox, as moth, as owl, as trout, Étain's is a naturally ecumenical humanity.

As is Conaire's. Ecumenical with all that he inwardly is, it comes naturally to Conaire to be ecumenical with everything around him.

Totemic as they are to each other, everything we say of Conaire we can say of the bird. That's why his reign is called

The Birdreign

Ingcél and Fer Rogain talk about it in an early medieval text called *Togail Bruidne Dá Derga*, or *The Destruction of Dá Derga's Hostel*:

> '*Cid ahé libse a flaithius ind fir sin i tír nÉrenn?*' *or Ingcél.*
> '*Is maith a flaith,*' *ol Fer Rogain.* '*Ní taudchaid nél tar gréin ó gabais flaith ó medón erraich co medón fogmair, ocus ní taudchaid banna drúchtae di feór co medón lai, ocus ní fascnan gaemgaeth cairchech cethrae co nónae, ocus ní foruich mac tibhri ina flaith tar ag fireand cacha indise ón chind mbliadnae co araill. Ocus ataat secht meic thiri i ngiallnai fri raigid ina thigseom fri coimét in rechtai sin ocus atá cúlaitiri iarna cúl .i. Macc Locc ocus is é taccair tar a cend hi tig Conaire. Is ina flaith is combind la cach fer guth araili ocus betis téta mendchrot ar febus na cána ocus in tsída ocus in chaínchomraic fil sethnu na Hérind. Is ina flaith ataat na trí bairr for Érind .i. barr dés ocus barr scoth ocus barr measa.*'

'What,' asked Ingcél, 'are the virtues of his reign in Ireland?'

'A good reign it is,' replied Fer Rogain. 'Since he became king no cloud covers the sun from the middle of spring until the middle of autumn and not a drop of dew evaporates from the grass till midday and no gust of wind shakes a cow's tail till evening and in any one year a wolf will take only one bull calf from an enclosure and in guarantee of this agreement seven wolves remain as hostages by the wall of his house and, by way of further assurance, Mac Locc pleads their case in Conaire's house. To his neighbour each man's voice is as melodious as the strings of harps and that because of the excellence of law and of peace and goodwill that is now to be found throughout Ireland. It is in Conaire's reign that we have the three crowns of Ériu, the crown of corn, the crown of flowers and the crown of acorns.'

How it was in Ireland during *Ind Énflaith*

during *The Birdreign*

FURTHER REFLECTIONS

Cormac and Conaire. Each in his own way, they undertake or rather they undergo the hazardous journey to Tara.

Dreamed by their people on to that road, each of them is a king in the making.

In the sense that it engages us in the roots of who we are, this road to our royalty is a root road, as it were an etymological road. Beset by our totem ancestors, whether wolf or bear or bird, it is a primary, if not primal, road. On it we are claimed as well by nature as by culture. On it we undergo our first shapeshiftingly insecure attempts to be human. To be totemically human, that is. For Cormac and Conaire on this road, safe assimilation to a totem animal outside themselves gives way to safe assimilation to animal nature in themselves. It is their attempt, in living it wholly, to bring the whole human psyche with them. That way, unlike Lughaidh mac Con, they won't be etymologically usurped.

Usurpation, totemic or otherwise, by animal nature from within, that is the hazard. Both Cormac and Conaire underwent and survived the hazard.

Realizing them vajrasatvically, making them vajrasatvically real, Cormac was struck by lightning and Conaire was made to pass through the fiercely destructive yet fiercely regenerating flames of the sepulchral bonfire.

Thinking of them, we can see that there is a higher totemism, the totemism of being assimilated not backwards to an archetype but forwards to a teleotype.

The word archetype is a compound of two Greek words, *arche,* meaning old in the creative sense of primary and original, and *tupos,* meaning a pattern of which copies are or can be made. Teleotype is also a compound of two Greek words, *teleos,* meaning perfect as applied to something fully realized and complete, and again *tupos.*

As fully realized human beings, royal in their natures before they were institutionally royal, Cormac and Conaire are teleotypes and, as such, we can aspire forward toward them, forward toward royal realization in ourselves on the day when, riding past it in Tara, the stone phallus will screech against our chariot axle.

After the depradations and dislocations wrought in Ireland by Cromwell, two Kerry poets, Aodhghán Ó Rathaille and Eoghan Ruadh Ó Suilleabháin, dreamed of a restoration of the old Catholic, Gaelic order.

After centuries of ecological havoc we need a restoration of

Ind Énflaith

To Plato I say:

An Énflaith not a Republic, a thing too unetymologically and exclusively human to bring out the best in us. It doesn't suit us. Worse, it doesn't suit the Earth. And that, in the end, must mean Hell-upon-Earth.

To St Augustine I say:

Blocc and Bluigne, the Druidic standing stones, have opened before us and we have passed through into a more or less druidic way of understanding ourselves and our world. In ourselves there is druidheacht. There is druidheacht in the world.

To Rousseau I say:

Listen to the screech out of Ireland. It is the screech of Fál, the stone phallus, announcing the universally ecumenical

Birdreign

To the blackbird who has just walked in through my open door and, having flown up onto it, stands unalarmed on a pile of books, among them a Cambridge Classics edition of *Oedipus Rex*, a king etymologically usurped – to him, the blackbird, I say:

that single screech of Fál is our universally ecumenical

Magna Carta

it is our universally ecumenical

Easter Proclamation

it is our universally ecumenical

Anthem

As for the feather the blackbird left behind – it could be a feather of

Maat

The goddess of Truth. Truth in the sense of

Right Cosmic Order

In our day it must mean what it once meant in Ireland:

A BIRDREIGN

A migration of the western mind from Thebes to Tara, from the reign of our secretly insurgent repressions in Thebes to a reign inwardly and outwardly ecumenical at Tara – that would be real progress, wouldn't it?

To Plato we say, come live in

The Birdreign

To Rousseau we say, come live in

The Birdreign

To Karl Marx we say, come live in

The Birdreign

River and star and archaeornis and ammonite and wolf and bear and crab and crow and lichen and louse and oatgrass, aurora and oak, everything included, the good weal is a

Commonweal

Weal and woe.
Not without woe the

Commonweal

But, as the old book has it:

Bid saineamail ind énflaith

Dolmen Love

GRÁINNE was betrothed to Fionn, a renowned warrior much older than she was. At a celebration in her father's house, Fionn the guest of honour, she challenged Diarmaid Ó Duibhne, a younger man and friend to Fionn, to elope with her. This he did, and so began a flight and a pursuit that crossed more boundaries, not all of them natural, than had ever been crossed before.

Some nights, taking refuge with the megalithic dead, they would sleep on dolmens.

Its sixty-ton capstone overgrown with a deep bed of heather and bilberry and bracken and grass and lichens and moss, no dolmen so suited and sheltered them as did the one called Labby Rock in Sligo. Down hill from Magh Tuired was the site of the great apocalyptic battle of Ireland's Dreamtime, the Tuatha Dé Danann, a good people, winning the day against the Fomorians, a recently arrived evil people.

Tonight more than ever Diarmaid and Gráinne are aware of the king and the queen megalithically buried beneath them.

Local lore has it that the king is none other than Nuada. King of the Tuatha Dé, he was slain by Balar of the evil eye in the great battle.

GR: By my count, this is the thirtieth dolmen we have slept on.

DI: A lot of sleep on top of a lot of death.

GR: A lot of love on top of a lot of death.

DI: I have a secret.

GR: Tell me.

DI: Passionately with you, always with you, on thirty dolmens with you, I have discovered a deep and delighted intimacy between love and death. In love tonight – there will be love tonight – how can there not be love tonight – in love tonight and every night we aren't only Diarmaid and Gráinne on top of dolmen death. Passion cremating us, we are the commingled royal ashes in the burial chamber beneath us.

GR: You speak what I know. What I came to know, the night I first set eyes on you.

DI: The surprise of it! The wonder of it!

GR: Tell me. Tell me what I know. What with you I know.

DI: Until I met you, until that first night that I lay down with you on that first dolmen, I had thought of death as the end of life. I being a warrior, I had thought of it as the spear-headed, sword-sided end of life. In battle, the bloody end of life. Now I know that it is what lifts love and life off the ground, as this dolmen does, lifting us up not on a bed of limp clothes but on a living springing bed of lichen and moss and mountain grass and bracken and bilberry and heather, the heather in flower and the bilberry in berry.

GR: As soon as we came out of the hazel wood today and we looked and we saw it, I knew it, and you knew it, no dolmen so great a wonder as this one.

DI: Give a poor upland tribe six stones, one of them an impossibly heavy stone of sixty or seventy tons, and ask them, or no, on pain of their survival demand of them that they build the most tremendous thing in the world, none so great as it anywhere ever before, none so great as it anywhere ever after, and that is what they did, giving unimaginable dignity to death and to life, the whole thing an eagle taking off into easy flight, or no, an eagle already in flight, effortlessly and unmovingly riding a gentle updraft into higher flight, its own delight its endless destination.

GR: I have a secret.

DI: Tell me.

GR: At the well the other day I met an old woman. 'What', I asked her, 'is happening in Ireland now?'

She looked surprised. So surprised, she looked at me even more surprised.

'You standing right here beside me,' she said, 'you standing in Ireland and you mean to tell me that you don't know what is happening right now in Ireland? Doesn't everyone everywhere know what is happening in Ireland now. Haven't you heard the hounds in the night? And the hunting horns at dawn, haven't you heard them?' 'Those hounds and horns, tell me about them,' I asked. 'Already all over the country they have been heard,' she said. 'Already it is called the greatest pursuit that ever was in the world, Fionn the old man, Fionn and his instincts, Fionn and his hounds, pursuing the eloped lovers, Diarmaid and Gráinne. Already 'tis as big as a folktale, already 'tis as big as history itself, Fionn the old man, when he does sleep, sleeping on the cold, wet earth, but the eloped and still eloping lovers, they sleeping embraced, more than embraced, on dolmens, and every tribe no matter where wanting them to sleep on their dolmen.'

'Why,' I asked her, 'why would they want the eloped lovers to sleep on top of their dead ancestors?'

'Something about it being good for the land,' she said. 'Something about it giving life to the land, and to the ancestors. Something about it giving life, giving dolmen life, to the living and the dead.'

DI: I sense it. There is something you aren't telling me.

GR: They will die.

DI: Did she say how?

GR: She did.

DI: How?

GR: I saw it in a dream. I saw the boar. When I saw him first, standing so still on a flat-topped mountain, I thought it was a dolmen. But the dolmen bristled. Bristled and charged, ripping the man, and news of it ripped the woman.

DI: Fionn and his wolfhounds behind us, a dream-big boar in front of us, and our love-bed a dolmen.

GR: Forget the hounds, forget the boar. Of the dolmen you said that its destination is its own endless delight.

DI: There is something you know.

GR: Tell me what I know.

DI: Having lain with me you know that there is unrestrainable running towards each other in love. In it also is elopement and pursuit.

GR: Fionn and his wolfhounds.

DI: No, I am not talking about Fionn and his wolfhounds. Nor am I talking about a boar sharpening his instincts to slaughter. I am talking rather about the frightful impulses that emerge in a warrior in battle. They emerged in me. And if they emerged in me in battle, in the blind passions of battle, why can they not also emerge in love? They frighten me. Only they frighten me. It is why I hesitated when you challenged me to elope with you. I knew we could elope from Fionn and your father, but what of those impulses, could we elope from them?

GR: Have we eloped from them?

DI: No.

GR: How close behind us are they?

DI: I embrace you with them.

GR: But no harm has come to me. Only the best love I have ever known has come to me. Climbing mountains with you, crossing rivers with you, eating wild roots with you, lying down tonight on this dolmen with you, no other woman in Ireland is so much a woman as I am. Look up at them. The shining stars approve of me. They approve of us. I know it. I know it. With you I have never been in danger so great and yet I have never been so safe. Safe at the beginning of passion, in the middle of passion, and at the screaming, collapsing end of passion. It is true what the old woman said. With you, Diarmaid Ó Duibhne, with you on dolmens all over Ireland, with you on bare Poll na Brón, we have been good for the land, we have been good for our ancestors buried with their household things and digging things and killing things beneath us. And tonight, Diarmaid Ó Duibhne, my dangerous, safe man, even if tonight be the night when our dolmen turns boar and tusks us, tonight, before anything else, we will be good for each other, and for the king and queen beneath us. In us the megalithic and the Celtic peoples are meeting, in love, in dolmen love, in love dying down into this dolmen, dying down into the land. How else can the dead live again? How else, except in us now, can the megalithic king and queen live again? How else can the land live again?

For the rest our legend will look after us. Fionn and his wolfhounds behind us, a dream-big boar in front of us, with us something new came into the world, with us death as an enrichment of life and love came into the world, with us dolmen love came into the world. Let it come into it, Diarmaid Ó Duibhne. Let it come into it one last time.

A Christian Orpheus

WE KNOW him as St Ciarán of Saighir, one of Ireland's earliest Christians. It is said that he met St Patrick in Rome. Sensing a kind of saintly outlandishness in him, Patrick gave him a hand-bell, telling him to go home and set up a monastery wherever it rang unrung. It rang, unrung, in a wilderness scarce in everything except savagery.

Reverent remembrance, already old in the eight century, loves his story:

> The blessed Ciarán took up his habitation like a hermit in the waste, for all about was a waste and tangled woodland. He began to build his little cell of mean stuff, and that was the beginning of his monastery. Afterwards a settlement grew up by God's gift and the grace of the holy Ciarán. And all these have the one name, Seir.
>
> Now when he came there he sat down under a tree in the shade of which was a boar of savage aspect. The boar seeing a man for the first time fled in terror, but afterwards, being tamed by God, it returned like a servant to the man of God. And that boar was Ciarán's first disciple and served him like a monk in that place. For the boar immediately fell to before the eyes of the man of God and with his teeth stoutly severed branches and grasses to serve for the building of the cell. For there was none with the holy man of

God in that place. For he had fled to the waste from his own disciples. Then came other animals from the lairs of the waste to the holy Ciarán, a fox, a badger, a wolf and a stag. And they abode with him as tame as could be. For they followed the commands of the holy man in all things like monks.

One day the fox, being more subtle and full of guile than the rest, stole the slippers of the abbot, the holy Ciarán, and turning false to his vow carried them off to his old earth in the waste, designing to devour them there. And when the holy Ciarán knew of this, he sent another monk or disciple, the badger, to follow the fox into the waste and to bring his brother back to his obedience. So the badger, who knew the ways of the woods, immediately obeyed the command of his elder and went straight to the earth of Brother Fox. He found him intent on eating his lord's slippers, so he bit off his ears and his brush and tore out his hairs. And then he constrained him to accompany him to his monastery that there he might do penance for his theft. So the fox, yielding to force, came back with the badger to his own cell to the holy Ciarán, bringing the slippers still uneaten. And the holy man said to the fox: 'Wherefore, brother, hast thou done this evil thing, unworthy of a monk? Behold! Our water is sweet and common to all. And if thou hadst a desire of thy natural craving to eat flesh, the omnipotent God would have made thee flesh of the bark of trees at our prayer.' Then the fox, craving forgiveness, did penance fasting, and ate nothing until the holy man commanded. Then he abode with the rest in familiar converse.

Afterwards his own disciples and many others from every side gathered about the holy Ciarán in that place; and there a famous monastery was begun. But the tame creatures aforesaid abode there all his life, for the holy elder had pleasure to see them.

What a charming end to our battle with the Beast in ourselves and in the world! Ciarán and badger and boar and fox and stag and wolf singing matins together in a little thatched church in the wilderness, its door antler high and wide to nature inside and outside us:

> *Caeli enarrant gloriam Dei, et opera manuum ejus annuntiat*
> *firmamentum*

Singing lauds together:

> *Cantate Domino canticum novum, cantate Domino omnis*
> *terra.*
> *Cantate Domino, et benedicite nomini ejus: annunciate de die*
> *in diem salutare ejus.*
> *Annunciate inter gentes gloriam ejus, in omnibus populos*
> *mirabilia ejus …*

Singing nones together:

> *Jubilate Deo omnis terra: servite Domino in laetitia.*
> *Introite in conspectu ejus, in exultatione.*

Singing vespers together:

> *In illa die stillabunt montes dulcedinem et colles fluent lac et*
> *mel, alleluia, Euouae.*

It must be that Ciarán was at ease with animal nature in himself, else the boar-brutal, fox-vicious, stag-shy animals of the wilderness wouldn't have been so happy to sing *Nunc Dimittis*, bringing compline to an end, with him:

> *Nunc dimittis servum tuum, Domine, secundum verbum*
> *tuum in pace, quia viderunt oculi mei salutare tuum, quod*
> *parasti ante faciem omnium populorum, lumen ad revela-*
> *tionem gentium et gloriam plebis tuae, Israel.*

Bethlehem and Saighir or, as it is phonetically rendered in the text, Seir.

Over the centuries, Christians have become used to Bethlehem, to the idea of two domesticated animals, an ox and an ass, breathing warmth on a wonder-child lying in their manger.

But what of Seir? What of two savage animals, a wolf and a boar, what of them singing matins? What of them, before they go back to their monastic cells at night, singing Simeon's Song of Salvation:

> Lord, now lettest thou thy servant depart in peace, according to thy word: For mine eyes have seen thy salvation, Which thou hast prepared before the face of all people; A light to lighten the Gentiles, and the glory of thy people Israel.

A wolf! With predatory eyes! Breaking off from the hunt and seeing salvation – with those eyes?

Is this the messianic outcome of history and of creation as the Bible foresees it?

Is it that, here in Seir, Ciarán and the animals are already living that outcome?

The wolf also shall dwell with the lamb …

The lion shall eat straw like the ox.

The sucking child shall play on the hole of the asp and the weaned child shall put his hand in the cockatrice's den.

There will be no hurt on God's holy mountain.

A sense I have is that there is something quite different going on in Seir.

The sense I have of him is that Ciarán is a Christian Orpheus.

In his nature, in all of it, not just in part of it, he has emerged into the Orphic note and that is why the animals, savage like the boar and shy like the stag, are happy to sing it with him.

Not that it is all Orphic plain sailing in Seir.

When it does eventually happen, the regression, while comic, is serious, especially so in the case of the badger.

One day there it was, another bowl of vegetable soup set before the fox. Looking down into it, his mouth wearied and watered for flesh, for bleeding, hot raw flesh deep as his teeth. In his mind he had a hare in sight, his nostrils drinking her smell. Mightily he resisted the impulse and soon again he was calm, the soup, as it so often did, tasting like penance. Next day, passing his cell door, he saw that the abbot had left his slippers outside to dry in the sun. Thinking that he might find the taste of hide in the leather, he yielded to his instincts and made off with them and before he knew what was what he was back to his old ways in his old earth in the wood.

No sooner had the badger entered the earth than he too regressed, turning snarlingly savage, biting off the fox's ears, biting off his tail, tearing the fur from shoulder and belly. Never, during all those years in the wild, had he fought as ferociously as he did now, in the interest, seemingly, of monastic law and order.

So what then of the Orphic note? Does it exist? And if it does, are there people who in their very being become it? Is it immanent in all of nature, in rocks, in animals, in stars? Is the universe but a blossoming of it? Is it an astronomical exuberance of it? Is it the eternal divine silence in its adventure into sound that we are talking about? Is that what the Orphic note is, the sound of the eternal divine silence, that sound solid in rocks, stellar in stars? And when someone reverts from sound to silence, will wolf and badger and boar and fox and stag, as by impulsion from an awakened instinct that lessens established instincts, will they turn on their trails, following what is now their chief desire, to be sym-phonic with it?

To be symphonic with it in Ciarán of Seir is to be symphonic with it in themselves. In Seir, to be symphonic with it as sound is to be symphonic with it as silence. The boar and the stag who were symphonic with it as sound at matins, at lauds, at nones, at vespers and at compline, were symphonic and maybe homeophonic with it as the eternal divine silence.

It should be remembered as a great day – the day a hand-bell rang unrung in Ireland.

And Seir? Seir is the bindu, the centre of the mandala, the

place of universal emergence and return.

And Ciarán? As Ogma once was, Ciarán is now the philosophical question. To understand him is ultimate understanding of all things.

In Ireland, St Ciarán's Christianity preceded the Christianity of St Patrick. Isn't it time we gave it precedence in other than a temporal sense? In this of course, even in thinking about it, we must remember that it was Patrick who gave the hand-bell to Ciarán, and so, in fairness, the question of precedence must remain undecided. What is important is that, having been a founding bell, the hand-bell could be the bell of refounding.

Christianity isn't only a morality that has its source in divine command.

As well as so much else that it presumably was, at Seir Christianity was the lived apprehension of unity in plurality out of which an ecumenical morality prospered. Ecumenical not just among human beings of different persuasions and languages. Ecumenical across all boundaries, among all species living and extinct, among all worlds visible and invisible.

And as for what happened to Brother Fox and Brother Badger, well, yes, it happens to individuals, it happens to tribes, it happens to civilizations and we only have to look at the one we live in to know that it happens to worlds.

As Christ born on the bestial floor does, as Christ in the Canyon does, Ciarán of Saighir suits our world.

Our Song of Ascent into Ireland

ALREADY, even as I was being baptised at our well, at Cle-bach Well, by Patrick, I knew that Christianity wouldn't suit me. It didn't. But it was all of twenty three years before my father came towards me in a dream. Death hadn't diminished him. Still a great pagan, a great druid, he commanded me to go home to Cruachan.

To Cruachan of the fifty green burial mounds, under each of them not just the remains of ancient kings and queens.

To Cruachan of the thorn bushes, many of them growing alone.

To Cruachan of the great pagan rites righting us to Sun and Moon, righting us to the Earth, and to ourselves.

To Cruachan of the standing stones.

To Cruachan of the skald crows, one of them red-mouthed.

To Cruachan where, on May morning, the herdsmen bleed their cattle on the grave mounds, Megalithic and Celtic, leaving them as red as the reddest sunrise.

To Cruachan of the teamed horses.

To Cruachan of the scything chariots.

To Cruachan of the ringforts, the paths to them as unexpected as folktales, their gates and their doors as deep as folktales.

To Cruachan of the Phantom: nights there are when her screech quenches every hearth-fire in Ireland.

To Cruachan of Uaigh na gCat.

Walking past it, a stranger might think that Uaigh na gCat was yet another underground cave in limestone land.

To pagans it is the entrance to the Otherworld. To Christians, who avoid it, it is the hell-mouth, a way out for all kinds of terrors and horrors, all of them devilish.

This is the nineteenth year that I have lived in a hut beside it.

Sometimes, without my being able to do anything about it, it is a fissure inside my own mind. A fissure through which nightmares not mine emerge leaving me not able to see out through my eyes next day.

The second time he walked towards me in a dream my father looked dilapidatedly Christian. Always, he said, there must be someone who sits by the hell-mouth. Someone who is it. Always there must be someone who is surrogate in this for all humanity, suffering our nightmares. Else, no one would sleep. And that, quite soon, would be the end of us.

Who was he talking about, I wondered? Was he talking about me in my hell-mouth hut or was he talking about Jesus in Gethsemane?

To be the hell-mouth to humanity? To the Earth? To all things?

The very thought of it very nearly tripped me headlong back into Christianity.

So what, I asked myself, if Christianity doesn't suit me?

A thin wind from the north on a night when I have no firewood, that doesn't suit me. A fox killing my five laying hens on a day when I have nothing to eat, that doesn't suit me. People avoiding me because I live as I do, that doesn't suit me.

How well, I asked myself, does my nature suit me? How well does my nightmaring mind suit me?

That something doesn't suit me isn't a good enough reason

to walk away from it and this, I thought, is as true of Christianity as it is of my nature.

If I couldn't be a Christian monk with Ciarán in Saighir could I be a Christian druid with the Sun and the Moon and the Earth and the Wind and the Rain here in Cruachan? Could I be a pagan Christian?

The wonder was that wolf and stag and fox and badger and boar had helped Ciarán to build his monastery. To him, they were his monks. That was why I went there, only in the end to see my father coming towards me.

It hardly matters now. But Christians are right in one thing. At the dead of night, not dead here, Uaigh na gCat is a hell-mouth not an entrance to a marvellous Otherworld.

It is not called Uaigh na gCat, the Cave of the Cats, for nothing.

Having as much ferocity as they need, having whatever shape and size they need, three Terrors, catlike in their stealth, will emerge and, just to prove to themselves that they can do it, they will leave people unable ever again to inhabit themselves.

It is a question that has settled on me. On bad nights I ask, how inwardly habitable are we? Can we inhabit ourselves in all of what we are? Are there worse things than putting out to sea on an outgoing tide in a small coracle? Is it worse to put out into ourselves? How seaworthy is the coracle? How sleepworthy is the self? How dreamworthy is it? How mareworthy, how nightmareworthy, is it? Just think of how many times on a bad night we are alarmed back into waking. Into terrified waking. Supposing we weren't alarmed back? Supposing we couldn't wake up? Supposing we couldn't come out and stay out of our nightmaring minds?

On bad nights, here at the hell-mouth, I don't wake up.

And what is worst of all, the nightmares seem so alien to me, so not mine. It wouldn't surprise me if you told me that in the dead of night my head is a boar's head or a bear's head. And that is why I am so troubled by our Celtic Song of Ascent into Ireland. Setting his right foot on a south-western shore, Amhairghin Glúngheal sang it:

Am gaeth i mmuir
Am tond trethan
Am fuaim mara
Am dam secht ndrenn
Am séig i n-aill
Am dér gréne
Am cáin
Am torc ar gail
Am hé i llind
Am loch i mmaig
Am brí dánae
Am gai i fodb feras fechtu

I am a wind in the sea
I am a sea-wave upon the land
I am the roar of ocean
I am a stag of seven fights
I am a hawk on a cliff
I am a tear-drop of the sun
I am fair
I am a boar for valour
I am a salmon in a pool
I am a lake in a plain
I am the excellence of arts
I am a spear waging war with plunder

Sing this Song of Ascent into Ireland in Ireland's hell-mouth and what will it sound like? Magnified in the caverns of the Earth, what will it sound like?

I am not saying that the song is a delusion. I know to my cost that it isn't. Already in the not so deep places of our minds there is no boundary between us and the stag of seven fights, between us and the hawk. A little deeper and there is no boundary between us and the salmon. Deeper still and there is no boundary between us and the wind, between us and the wave.

It was in and from these deep places that Ciarán lived. He lived boundlessly, badger and boar and fox and stag and wolf working with him, singing matins and lauds and vespers and compline with him.

Would that my oldest and deepest instincts would sing matins with me. Above all, would that the instincts I share with badger and boar would sing compline with me, giving me a quiet night and a perfect end

Nunc dimittis servum tuum, Domine, secundum verbum tuum in pace, quia viderunt oculi mei salutare tuum ...

Ciarán at compline I think of. Amhairghin Glúngheal climbing a shingle shore I think of.

All that Amhairghin Glúngheal says he is, I instinctively am.

Now, at last, it is how I understand myself. It is why I endure myself, living, not sure of myself, from day to day.

Expecting less of myself than my father did, it is what I stumbled into and cannot now get out of.

Inland, here in Cruachan of the hell-mouth, I am the shadow side of our ascent into Ireland.

There is though another way of putting it.

In consequence of a victory secured with iron urns we, the Irish, are now the dominant people on this island. We believe in this world and in a marvellous Otherworld but we have neither a real nor an abiding sense of an underworld. That is a poverty and so, as well as suffering an extension to the geography of the Irish world I am suffering an extension to the geography of the Irish mind. The underworld is inside us as well as outside us.

There is something I know. If we, the Irish, are to become a great people there are some last things that we must undergo. All on my own, without iron, I am undergoing one of them.

Scelec

THEY ARE savageries of serrated, jagged rock rising out of the ocean. If sharks were as big as islands, you would think they were shark fins, the sharks circling before moving in for their mouthfuls. If the ocean could snarl as a stoat does, you would say, that is it, that is the ocean showing its eyeteeth.

Over a thousand years ago, believing in a god who was willing to hang for them, a group of Christian monks rowed themselves out here to hang with him, vertiginously so, building a constellation of stone igloos for themselves on an exposed shoulder of one of these precipices six-hundred feet above the uncovenanted sea. The other yet more serrated yet more jagged precipice they left to the sea birds, as much of it as white with their droppings then as it is now.

The danger out here is that you would one night ship your oar and fall in with nature and now instead of thinking of Christ as Lamb of God you would think of Him as Gannet of God, as Crab of God, as Lobster of God or, in extreme regression, as Shark of God.

Extremest perfection out here was the unthinking suddenness with which a gannet in high, inspecting flight would fold its wings and turn itself into a beaked spear diving upon a mackerel in the sea. Sometimes it would be a hail shower of gannets diving innumerably upon a shoal of mackerel, every splash a perfect kill.

The monks looked, and saw, and maybe one day one of them wondered, what compared to this that we see is our persistent yet always inadequate aspiration to moral perfection?

And yet there is perfection in how they built their igloos, laying stone upon dry stone, the circular wall graduating into a conical roof, the whole thing as waterproof as a gannet's egg.

I imagine a monk who believes that in coming to Scelec he has returned to the egg, to the igloo-egg, out of which, warmed by God's grace, he will one day emerge in Christlikeness. In the meantime he falls in every morning adding stone step to stone step in an ascent from sea to summit. Climbing it some nights, it is an asent from crab to Cancer, from plaice lying camouflaged and flat on the seafloor to Pisces among the stars.

Already there were people in the mainland who said they could see the souls of the Irish dead ascending this path on their way out into eternity. And once it happened: climbing with their mixed catch at nightfall, a crew of monks, all three of them, were suddenly not their full selves. Suddenly, they were as transparent as ghosts to their own Last Judgment.

That is how it was out here. Whatever your bulk against God and against nature, you'd be stripped out here. And the ones who did best were the ones who soonest learned to lie licken-low. But, stonemasons all of them, they would often feel that this, their most successful strategy, neither circled nor squared with their will to perfection.

It was troublesome. Giving way under the strain, a novice brake out and, untypically for him, he didn't hold back: it is no small thing, he raged, to do as well as nature does in the flower of a furze, in the snarl of a stoat, in the flight and dive of a gannet, but the moral equivalent of such perfection will make us inhuman. It is out of order. It is sacrilegious.

It worked. Sixty years later, grown old in the service of God, he talks to a similarly troubled novice. 'We live', he says, 'on a high, precipitous peak.

'One false step up here and you could soon find yourself drowning not just in your mortal body but in your immortal soul. Look at us older monks,' he says. 'Lowering our sights, we no longer seek moral perfection. For the reason that it is hospitable to moral failure we have settled for moral success.'

And yet it isn't a sin against the astrological night sky to think that this cluster of igloos is a constellation of igloos. Place a lighted candle in every door on a calm night and, if they looked up to take a stellar reading, fishermen who had been overtaken by darkness might for the moment think that this indeed was a new constellation and that they, although lost, were the first to set mortal eyes on it.

But then saying mass the next day, the abbot, while consciously intending to say *Agnus Dei*, might by a slip of the tongue say *Cancer Dei*. That right there at the heart of divine redemption was the most hideous of precipices, plunging all the way down from Lamb of God to Crab of God, plunging all they way from down from Lamb of God to circling Shark of God.

Thinking of those monks of Scelec I think of a poem called 'Hawk Roosting' by Ted Hughes:

> I sit in the top of the wood, my eyes closed.
> Inaction, no falsifying dream
> Between my hooked head and hooked feet:
> Or in sleep rehearse perfect kills and eat.
>
> The convenience of the high trees!
> The air's buoyancy and the sun's ray
> Are of advantage to me;
> And the earth's face upward for my inspection.
>
> My feet are locked upon the rough bark.
> It took the whole of Creation
> To produce my foot, my each feather:
> Now I hold Creation in my foot
>
> Or fly up, and revolve it all slowly
> I kill where I please because it is all mine.
> There is no sophistry in my body:
> My manners are tearing off heads –

The allotment of death,
For the one path of my flight is direct
Through the bones of the living.
No arguments assert my right:

The sun is behind me.
Nothing has changed since I began.
My eye has permitted no change.
I am going to keep things like this.

Christianity has it that the world is in the palm of God's hand. Here we are told that the hawk has locked his talons upon the whole of creation.

Christianity has it that Love makes the stars and the world go round. Here we are told that the hawk is *Primum Mobile*, revolving the whole world slowly to nothing better than predatory purpose.

Christianity has it that the world is at home in the all-seeing, foreseeing, providential eye of God. Here we are told that it has come to an evolutionary full stop in the eye of the hawk, an eye never in the least bit blinded by the glaucoma of conscience or remorse.

Thoughts a monk might think as he sits on a precipice in the Atlantic eating boiled crab claws for supper.

To get to the mouth-watering muscle that opened and closed the claw he has to shatter its pink, protective shell between two stones.

'My table manners', this monk might say, 'are shattering crab claws.' Claws that had closed on putrid left-overs lying on the bottom, that had closed cannibalistically on their own kind.

And the monk knows that there is as little conscience in his own mouth-water as there is in the claw-muscle he is eating.

Also, as he sits there murdering the muscle into himself, he has no choice but to acknowledge that the teeth of a carnivore have beaten the Beatitudes to a place in his head. Indeed, whenever he does so, it is through his at other times shearing and chewing dentition that he speaks the Beatitudes:

Blessed are the poor in spirit: for theirs is the kingdom of
heaven.

Blessed are they that mourn: for they shall be comforted.

Blessed are the meek: for they shall inherit the earth.

Blessed are they which do hunger and thirst after righteousness: for they shall be filled.

Blessed are the merciful: for they shall obtain mercy.

Blessed are the pure in heart: for they shall see God.

Blessed are the peacemakers: for they shall be called the
children of God.

Blessed are they which are persecuted for righteousness'
sake: for theirs is the kingdom of heaven.

Blessed are ye, when men shall revile you, and persecute
you, and shall say all manner of evil against
you falsely, for my sake.

To the hawk, whose right to his manners isn't established by argument, these nine means of entering into blessedness are sophistries.

To the hawk, Christianity in its doctrinal and sacramental entirety would be a bad dream, a falsifying dream, interrupting the instinctive free-flow between his hooked head and his hooked feet.

An attitude that MacMorris in *Henry V* would enthusiasti-cally endorse. Exasperated by the niceties of bookish theoric in military matters, he goes out declaring:

There is works to be done and throats to be cut.

On a calm, clear, August day out there on Scelec a single seagull's scream could slice open your Christian, meek mind all the way down to where the hawk's song of himself is your song of yourself. In sleep at that depth we too rehearse perfect kills and we eat.

Jesus crossed the Kedron into that depth, a depth common to human and hawk, and Christians believe that He redeemed it, with the result that a day foreseen long ago is our day now:

The wolf also shall dwell with the lamb, and the leopard shall lie down with the kid; and the calf and the young lion and the fatling together; and a little child shall lead them. And the cow and the bear shall feed; their young ones shall lie down together: and the lion shall eat straw like the ox.

A day yet more marvellous. Day when:

The sucking child shall play on the hole of the asp, and the weaned child shall put his hand in the cockatrice's den.

Day when:

They shall not hurt nor destroy in all God's holy mountain: for the earth shall be full of the knowledge of the Lord, as the waters cover the sea.

And there they therefore are, three small boats in the sea, at every oar a cowled monk. All around them a hail shower of gannets is diving into the sea, every splash a perfect kill.

splash

        splash   splash

     splash   splash

      splash   splash

         splash

A constellation of killing all around them, these Christians continue to row. Where others would see an eyetooth of snarling nature they see Christian aspiration rising up seven hundred feet out of the Atlantic. Seeking nearness to God, they will settle on a high shoulder of it and last thing every night at compline they will remember Simeon.

In his gospel, St Luke tells us that Simeon was a devout and a just man and it had been revealed to him by the Holy Ghost that he wouldn't taste of death before he had seen the Messiah, the Christos, the Anointed One of God, bringer of salvation to the whole world. One day, when he was well stricken in years,

Simeon was in the Temple in Jerusalem. A man and a woman came in and when the woman opened her shawl revealing the child she was carrying, Simeon looked at him and instantly he knew that this was Him, the Lord's Anointed, the Christ. What Simeon then said would soon become known as 'Simeon's Canticle' and it was this, in visionary identification with him, that the Scelec monks would sing last thing every night high up there in their dry stone oratory under the stars.

They would sing it in Latin:

Nunc dimittis servum tuum, Domine, secundum verbum tuum in pace, quia viderunt oculi mei salutare tuum, quod parasti ante faciem omnium populorum, lumen ad revelationem gentium, et gloriam plebis tuae, Israel.

In English it reads:

Lord, now lettest thou thy servant depart in peace, according to thy word: For mine eyes have seen thy salvation, Which thou hast prepared before the face of all people; A light to lighten the Gentiles, and the glory of thy people Israel.

The wonder of it, to retire to sleep only after you have seen your salvation.

And yet more wonderful: that salvation they sang between the hooked head and the hooked feet of the hawk.

There too is where the abbot, soon to be killed in a Viking raid, will say Mass, a few hours later, in the dark before dawn.

His chasuble is cut from an old sail many times unfurled far out at sea.

Emblazoned on it is his Christian faith in a successful outcome to history. Heraldically audacious, it depicts a sucking child playing at the hole of an asp and a weaned child putting his hand in a cockatrice's den.

Sanctus, he sings –
Sanctus, they all sing –

Sanctus, sanctus, sanctus, Dominus Deus Sabaoth, pleni sunt caeli et terra gloria tua.

No slip of the tongue this morning.

This morning, out here on the last precipice of the world, the hawk is having a hard time of it keeping things his way. This morning history is unhooking its head, is unhooking its feet.

Or is it?

It is Anno Domini 824 and under that date the *Annals of Inisfallen* has this among other things to say:

Scelec do orgain do gentib ocus Etgal do brith i mbrait co nerbail gorta leo.

Scelec was plundered by the heathens and Etgal was carried off into captivity, and he died of hunger in their hands.

And so, another constellation, this one of blood splashed upon Christian aspiration out at sea:

splash

splash

splash

splash

splash   splash

splash

splash

splash

splash   splash

splash

And the name of this new constellation?

Am Séig i n-Aill

That, or

The Hawk's Manners

In time, a generation of monks will rededicate their precipice to Michael the Archangel and with this they will have regressed from the Orphic note to the sword.

For now at least, our hope of a second Saighir, of a Saighir at sea, is lost.

For now our hope of an Énflaith, with gannet and crab and shark and seal at sea, is lost.

AFTERTHOUGHTS

Can there be a religion that doesn't falsify nature?

Can there be a religion that doesn't falsify the shark closing in for its mouthful?

Can there be a religion that neither falsifies nor repudiates the might-is-right tyranny of Tyrannosaurus Rex?

Can there be a religion that doesn't falsify the sexual instinct in ourselves?

Reclining as opulently as he does in his dolphomorphic boat, its topsail a spreading grapevine, is that what Dionysus is, god in and of nature unrestrained and uncontaminated by moral demand, 'is' uncontaminated by 'ought'?

We look at him, this god who reveals himself to us at the bottom of the pre-Christian chalice and we think, yes, he is the god who delights in things as they are not in things as they ought to be.

This brings us back to Fionn mac Cumhaill, he, in his own words, delighting in the music of what happens.

An tráth do mhair Fionn's and Fhiann,
   dob ansa leo sliabh ná cill;
ba binn leo-san fuighle lon,
   gotha na gclog leo níor bhinn.

In their day Fionn and the Fianna
delighted in the blackbird calling them to immanence,
not in the Christian bell calling them to transcendence.

For the Christian on Scelec of course it did not come down to a choice between the blackbird and the bell. Nor did it come down to a choice between chalices, Dionysian and Christian.

Some of the most numinous poems in old Irish testify to the delight of Christian hermits in the call of a blackbird heard over water or from nearby willow, two of which I recall:

> *Int én bec*
> *ro léic feit*
> *do rinn guip*
>   *glanbuidi;*
> *fo-ceird faíd*
> *ós Loch Láig*
> *lon do chraib*
>   *charnbuidi.*

*

> *Int én gaires asin tsail*
> *álainn guilbnén as glan gair:*
>   *rinn binn buide fir duib druin*
>   *cas cor cuirther, guth ind luin.*

If the perfect, mellow, self-marvelling quavers that issue from the blackbird's yellow are the signature of nature, revealing what nature essentially is, then, if we need it at all, our religion must be correspondingly mellow, praise of all things its only concern, all its psalms *Exultets*.

If the tyrannical, red roar of Tyrannosaurus Rex is the signature of nature, revealing what it essentially is, then to seek redemption in nature is to seek redemption in something that needs, itself, to be redeemed, and so it is that Christ's Jurassic screech from the cross is unexceptionally symphonic with the music of what happens.

A few miles over the sea from Scelec, in Inis Dairbhre, on rocks of the same geological formation and age, are the fossilized footprints of a tetrapod left on a mudflat three hundred and eighty million years ago when Ireland was in two halves south of the equator. In that tetrapod, lungs have replaced gills and fins have become feet. In him life has emerged from the sea. In him life is on the move, but to where? Water in those three hundred and eighty million year old footprints mirrors a vapour trail in a modern sky. It isn't, but it could be, the vapour trail of a fighter jet called Tornado or Harrier.

'*Am gaeth i mmuir,*' the fighter pilot might sing:

Am gaeth i mmuir
Am tond trethan
Am fuaim mara
Am dam secht ndrenn
Am séig i n-aill ...

But it isn't only into a fighter pilot that the tetrapod has evolved. He has evolved into a poet in hawkish ventriloquy:

The sun is behind me.
Nothing has changed since I began.
My eye has permitted no change.
I am going to keep things like this.

This is a bigger defeat than his beheading for Orpheus.

So which will it be, the fossilized footprints and the vapour trail or the fossilized footprints, and those steep stone steps ascending from crab to Cancer, from plaice to Pisces?

And, as Dylan Thomas might say, they shall have stars, those monks ...

And they shall have stars at elbow and foot

And they shall have stars at elbow and foot

And they shall have stars at elbow and foot

As will Vikings.

As will the tetrapod, to a constellation mirrored in his own Devonian footprints.

And yet, and yet. Down from the footprints are two rock pools. I look down into them and I think, no, it is not for us to become stellar, it is for stars to become terrestrial.

And this brings us back to the fate of Orpheus in Greece.

Votaries of Dionysus that they were, did the Maenads tear Orpheus asunder because he would have falsified the earth, converting its miraculous savagery into docile sterility? Could there for them be anything so degrading and so sad as to see a lion eating straw like an ox or to hear a wolf singing compline with Ciarán? For them no Isaiah. For them the God who spoke to Job out of the whirlwind saying, 'Behold now behemoth, which I made with thee.' For them Blake who said:

> The roaring of lions, the howling of wolves, the raging of the stormy sea and the destructive sword are portions of eternity too great for the eye of man.

Didn't Dionysus himself become a lion, didn't he become a roaring portion of eternity to the pirates who would have restrained and chained him?

Better that than our calamitous biblical ambition to rule over and subdue all things.

It was deliberately not by a slip of His biblical tongue that his biblical God advised Job to abandon this, his biblical ambition:

> Canst thou draw out Leviathan with an hook? or his tongue with a cord which thou lettest down? Canst thou put an hook into his nose? or bore his jaw through with a thorn? Will he make many supplications unto thee? will he speak soft words unto thee? Will he make a covenant with thee? wilt thou take him for a servant forever? Wilt thou play with him as with a bird? or wilt thou bind him for thy maidens? Shall the companions make a banquet of him? shall they part him among the merchants? Canst thou fill his skin with barbed irons? or his head with fish spears? Lay thine hand upon him, remember the battle, do no more. Behold the hope of him is in vain: shall not one be cast down even at the sight of him?

Amhairghin's six questions.

Yahweh's fifteen questions.

Were Yahweh's fifteen questions the fifteen planks of the boat that St Fionán and his monks sailed to Scelec in?

St Ciarán and St Fionán, the one founding a monastery inland in Saighir, the other founding his monastery offshore on Scelec.

Is it inevitable that Christianity inland will be different from Christianity offshore? As different as the mellow voice of a blackbird from the mind-slicing scream of a gannet?

Not by a slip of the tongue but in a deliberate act of piety, can we say

Crab of God
Shark of God
Gannet of God

As Native Americans would, can we be Christian crab-dreamers, Christian shark-dreamers, Christian gannet-dreamers, Christian behemoth-dreamers, Christian Leviathan-dreamers, crab and shark and gannet and behemoth and Leviathan giving us the medicine of not being superior to the one world soul.

I think of something Yeats said:

I know now that revelation is from the self, but from that age-long memoried self, that shapes the elaborate shell of the mollusc and the child in the womb, that teaches birds to make their nest; and that genius is a crisis that joins that buried self for certain moments to our trivial daily mind.

That the boat we might sail up Kenmare Bay in.

That the boat we might sail to Scelec in.

That the song our indigenous Orpheus might sing to us in Saighir.

The bell that rings unrung isn't of our trivial daily mind. It is of the age-long memoried self that remembers itself as a tetrapod crossing a Devonian mudflat.

Round the peninsula from his footprints are Amhairghin's footprints. The fin in them both means that they are to that extent identical.

The fin in them means that within themselves our feet are more precipitous than Scelec.

Having slipped himself, Oedipus knows.

Having heard Eurydice his wife wailing all the way back down into the underworld, Orpheus knows.

As for Amhairghin and Fionán, the one setting out inland and the other setting out seaward, our hope for them is that they also know.

The boar that Amhairghin is could charge straight into the spear that he is, and the sudden enclosure of Fionán's hands and feet in a bull's feet must mean that his ascent from plaice to Pisces is altogether more precipitous than he had bargained for.

On this ascent, until I have integrated all that I am, the bull I am is overhang, the salmon I am is overhand, the boar I am is overhang.

On the mystical ascent, even if I was Cancer, in that too I would overhang my ascending not-self.

Think how much Amhairghin Glúngheal would have learned had he attempted to ascend Scelec before he ascended Kenmare Bay.

To ascend Scelec is why someone who would reach Ireland would go back out a second time over nine waves.

Here we will do well to remember that Scelec Mór of the two unequal heights and Dá Chích Danann and Dá Chích na Morrígna are versions, offshore and insland, of each other, and so, whoever makes it on one of them has thereby made it on the other two. The extent to which Ollamh Fódhla made it between the Paps of Redmouthed Morrigu is the extent to which he made it on Scelec.

In Ollamh Fódhla we are still seeking to reach Ireland.

As we are in Conaire Mór walking naked to Tara, that is the hill of everyone's royalty.

Wolves seeking to lead him one way, wild horses another, the quest continues in Cormac mac Airt.

Splendid in himself and splendid as image and instance of what is royal, of what is regal, of what is sovereign in every one of us, Cormac was one day standing on the rampart wall in

Tara. He saw a sovereign lady coming towards him. She challenged him to a game of fidchel.

'What', Cormac asked, 'is the wager?'

'That you will know', she replied, 'only when you have won it or lost it.'

Cormac lost, and with that he found his sense of his royalty fading from him. While a glimmer of it yet remained to him, he commanded that his horses be yoked to his chariot. He rode south through the now desolate land. He crossed into another way, a perfect way, of seeing and knowing the world. The house he came to was perfect. It was thatched with feathers, no feather ruffled, all of them lying as perfectly layered upon it as his feathers lie upon a peregrine falcon's back. Inside, seated before a fidchel board, the pieces set, was the sovereign lady. Cormac won, and with that, to his surprise, he recovered his sense of his royalty.

'You were absent,' his wife said to him that night.

'I have suffered what will happen to people in Ireland in time to come,' Cormac said. 'They will lose their sense of their royalty. They won't know what Tara means. Their horses won't know the way to another way, to the perfect way, of seeing and knowing the world.'

Wolf-Time

I WAS a strange man and that's why I've lived alone, up here at the end of this valley, the mountains so high to the east and south and west of me that I'm cut off from the sun from October to March. It was mostly when I'd be out hunting that it would happen to me. Even if it was only a hare for my supper I was hunting, it could happen to me. I'd be walking along by a river maybe and an animal light that would never be morning would dawn in me and for as long as it lasted I would know what animals know. I swear to God, I would know what bushes know and I might as well give up then because, no matter how hungry I was, I couldn't level a gun at anything. It was like waking up to the wonder of things. And wonder is danger to how we normally are. It can bring down minds. Eyes and minds. And to say that it can bring down ways of seeing and knowing a world is to say that it can bring down worlds. It was wonder that brought down my first eyes and mind. It brought down my first world.

I was sitting at home one night. I needed to kill something, and so, when I heard the howl, I got up off my chair, I took down my gun and out I went. I had almost given up when, as I had hoped she would, she turned full on into the moon, and there they were, her brightened eyes giving her away. I fired and, two lopes later, a lurch, then lights going out. And at that very instant I knew what fox and badger knew. I knew what the hawthorn beside me knew. I knew I had killed Ireland's last wolf.

Back in my chair by my fire, I thought of a poem I had learned from a journeyman piper who would stay with me whenever he came this way. It is the poem of an outdoors man. Like myself, he'd be out of doors a lot even in winter. His talk is winter talk, and it wouldn't surprise me if he too didn't sometimes know what animals know, what bushes know:

Is úar geimred: at-racht gáeth;
éirgid dam díscir dergbáeth;
*   nocha te in-ocht in slíab slán,*
*   gé beith dam dían ac dordán.*

Ní thabair a tháeb re lár
dan Sleibe Cairn na comdál;
*   ní luga at-chluin ceól cúaine*
*   dam Cinn Eghte innúaire.*

Mise Cáilte, is Diarmat donn,
ocus Oscar áith étrom,
*   ro-choistmis re céol cúaine*
*   deired aidche adúaire …*

Céol Cúaine, that's what I had shot and killed. Wolf Music I had shot and killed, and Ireland and the Irish would never again be as real as they had been.

Even now I remember it, my night's work – eyes moon-brightened, a shot echoing off near cliffs and then, a little later, off far cliffs, two last lopes, a lurch, then lights going out.

And here I am eating hare soup, but never after that night was it given to me to know what hares know, to know what hawthorns know. Never again, my gun lying dead in my hand, has my next step been what it often was. But don't misunderstand me. None of this happened because I killed Céol Cúaine. I killed Céol Cúaine because I was already shrivelling into the man I now am. The wonder and surprise of things too much for me, I became normal. And my gun became normal, a thing to do things with. And Ireland also – whenever I cross out of this valley into Ireland, what I see is, it has become a place to do things in, so I come home.

It has come to this. Instead of high night-howling in Ireland, there it is, her skull on my dresser. It doesn't accuse me. It reminds me that when I am walking along by a river now every step is like the last step. The best I can hope for is that if it is a step in boggy ground it will fill with water and it will mirror the mountains. And even if it's already October and the mountains are cutting me off from the sun, that's something.

AFTERTHOUGHTS

Why is it that Irish historians will not talk at this level about Irish history? Why will they not ask the big questions?

Here, for example, is a big question: the shot that rang out one night in the Maam Valley in Connemara? What, compared to it, is the sailing away of the Irish chieftains from Ireland?

> The roaring of lions, the howling of wolves, the raging of the stormy sea and the destructive sword are portions of eternity too great for the eye of man.

There it is: one night in the Maam Valley we killed a portion of eternity. In killing it in our world we killed it in ourselves. Our world isn't so tremendous as it was. Nor are we.

Even though he doesn't say it in so many words, Blake will soon say that everything, big and small, is a portion of eternity.

If the doors of perception were cleansed everything would appear to man as it is, infinite.

Implying that, properly perceived, or should we say, implying that, apocalyptically perceived, a daisy is as ontologically stupendous as Tyger?

> Tyger! Tyger! burning bright
> In the forests of the night,

What immortal hand or eye
Could frame thy fearful symmetry?

In what distant deeps or skies
Burnt the fire of thine eyes?
On what wings dare he aspire?
What the hand dare seize the fire?

And what shoulder, and what art,
Could twist the sinews of thine heart?
And when thy heart began to beat,
What dread hand? And what dread feet?

What the hammer? What the chain?
In what furnace was thy brain?
What the anvil? What dread grasp
Dare its deadly terrors clasp?

When the stars threw down their spears
And water'd heaven with their tears,
Did he smile his work to see?
Did he who made the Lamb make thee?

Tyger! Tyger! burning bright
In the forests of the night,
What immortal hand or eye
Dare frame they fearful symmetry?

The native peoples of the Amazonian rainforest think of the jaguar as the night sun. In other words, what our sun does with its light, turning night into day, the jaguar does with his roar. Hear that roar and you will think that it is all of eternity, not just a portion of it, that has roared.

Walking one day into Lobo Canyon in New Mexico, D.H. Lawrence found himself walking into a gap, a void, in reality:

Climbing through the January snow, into the Lobo canyon
Dark grow the spruce-trees, blue is the balsam, water
    sounds still unfrozen, and the trail is still evident.

Men!
Two men!
Men! The only animal in the world to fear!

They hesitate.
We hesitate.
They have a gun.
We have no gun.

Then we all advance, to meet.

Two Mexicans, strangers, emerging out of the dark and
    snow and inwardness of the Lobo Valley.
What are they doing here on this vanishing trail?

What is he carrying?
Something yellow.
A deer?

Que tiene, amigo?
León –

He smiles, foolishly, as if he was caught doing wrong.
And we smile, foolishly, as if we didn't know.
He is quite gentle and dark-faced.

It is a mountain lion,
A long, long slim cat, yellow like a lioness.
Dead.

He trapped her this morning, he says, smiling foolishly.

Lift up her face,
Her round bright face, bright as frost.
Her round, fine-fashioned head, with two dead ears:
And stripes in the brilliant frost of her face, sharp, fine
    dark rays,
Dark, keen, fine rays in the brilliant frost of her face.
Beautiful dead eyes.
Hermoso es!

They go out towards the open;
We go on into the gloom of Lobo.
And above the trees I found her lair.
A hole in the blood-orange brilliant rocks that stick up,
    a little cave.
And bones, and twigs, and a perilous ascent.

So, she will never leap up that way again, with the yellow
    flash of a mountain lion's long shoot!
And her bright striped frost-face will never watch any
    more, out of the shadow of the cave in the blood-
    orange rock,
Above the trees of the Lobo dark valley mouth!

Instead I look out.
And out to the dim of the desert, like a dream, never real;
To the snow of the Sangre de Cristo mountains, the ice of
    the mountains of Picoris,
And near across at the opposite steep of snow, green trees,
    motionless, standing in snow, like a Christmas toy.

And I think in this empty world there was room for me
    and the mountain lion.
And I think in the world beyond, how easily we might
    spare a million or two humans
And never miss them.
Yet what a gap in the world, the missing white frost-face
    of that slim yellow mountain lion!

A pity the final misanthropy, if that is what it is, because we
only have to look, say, at Beethoven's thunderous face and we
know that the striped frost-face of the mountain lion is merely
cosmetic by comparison. And what of the sambhogakaya face of
an enlightened, lotus-enthroned Buddha? But no doubt about
it: the voidance, the making void, of Ireland's last wolf in the
Maam Valley and of the mountain lion in the Lobo Valley are
gaps, are ginunngagaps, in the world, and in ourselves.
    Cougar and jaguar.

Jaguar, the night sun: his screech is forked, red lightning lighting the piranha and anaconda night. So perfect is his savagery you'd be tempted to think of it as a liturgy of savagery, as a sanctity of savagery, as a *Missa Solemnis* of savagery. You'd be tempted to think of it as a Gothic cathedral of savagery that you dare not go into. Walking up the pungently claimed territorial aisle, more trail than aisle, you stand before the eternally frozen snarl that is its high altar and there, having confessed it, you are cleansed of your sin of Wordsworthian sentimentality regarding nature:

Three years she grew in sun and shower,
Then Nature said, 'A lovelier flower
On earth was never sown;
This Child I to myself will take;
She shall be mine, and I will make
A Lady of my own.

'Myself will to my darling be
Both law and impulse: and with me
The Girl, in rock and plain,
In earth and heaven, in glade and bower,
Shall feel an overseeing power
To kindle or restrain.

'She shall be sportive as the fawn
That wild with glee across the lawn
Or up the mountain springs;
And hers shall be the breathing balm,
And hers the silence and the calm
Of mute, insensate things.

'The floating clouds their state shall lend
To her; for her the willow bend;
Nor shall she fail to see
Even in the motions of the Storm,
Grace that shall mould the Maiden's form
By silent sympathy.

'The stars of midnight shall be dear
To her; and she shall lean her ear
In many a secret place
Where rivulets dance their wayward round,
And beauty born of murmuring sound
Shall pass into her face.

'And vital feelings of delight
Shall rear her form to stately height,
Her virgin bosom swell;
Such thoughts to Lucy I will give
While she and I together live
Here in this happy dell.'

Thus Nature spake – The work was done –
How soon my Lucy's race was run!
She died, and left to me
This heath, this calm, and quiet scene;
The memory of what has been
And never more will be.

Nature, forgetting her jaguar savageries, thinking she can do a better job than culture.

Back in the real world, here he comes, Bear singing, not his Whitmanian, but his Navajo, Song of Himself:

My moccasins are black obsidian
My leggings are black obsidian
My shirt is black obsidian
I am girded with a black arrowsnake
Black snakes go up from my head.

With zigzag lightnings darting from the end of my feet
      I step
With zigzag lightnings darting from my knees I step
With zigzag lightnings streaming from the tip of my tongue
      I speak.

Now a disk of pollen rests on the crown of my head
Grey arrowsnakes and rattlesnakes eat it

Black obsidian and lightning stream out of me in four ways
Where they strike the earth, bad things, bad talk do not
    like it
It causes the arrows to spread out
Long life, something frightful I am
Now I am.

There is danger where I move my feet
I am whirlwind
There is danger where I move my feet
I am a grey bear
When I walk, where I step, lightning flies from me
Where I walk, one to be feared I am
Where I walk, long life
One to be feared I am
There is danger where I walk.

The song of our Aillwee Cave Bear heard again in Ireland.
Look at him:

With zigzag lightnings darting from the end of his feet
    he walks
With zigzag lightnings darting from his knees he walks
With zigzag lightnings streaming from the tip of his tongue
    he speaks.

Walk among us, Bear.

Be what you are among us, Bear.

Be a portion of eternity or be the whole of eternity singing
your Song of Yourself among us, Bear

Where I walk, one to be feared I am
Where I walk, long life
One to be feared I am
There is danger where I walk.

Bear's Song. Amhrán Airt we might call it in Irish.

Amhrán Airt then and Céol Cúaine. Bear's Song and Wolf Music, and Fionn mac Cumhaill I imagine would insist that if we are to prosper as a people we must listen not just casually and as a matter of habit to the one and the other.

Fionn and his band of warrior-hunters, all of them poets, were sitting by the headwaters of the Blackwater in Sliabh Luachra, all of them at ease after a great battle fought and won yesterday and before what they were sure would be the greatest of all boar hunts proposed for the morrow.

'A question,' Fionn said. 'Each of us true to himself, what is the music we best like to hear in all the world?'

'The savage, beautiful music of an otter's face,' Oscar said.

'The music of hounds, far off and foamy, just before the stag turns and stands at bay,' Cáilte said.

'The screech the screech the screech the screech the squawk and the croak croak croak of a heron overflying a mirroring inlet of sea,' Diarmaid Ó Duibhne said.

'A victory of wild geese all broken up and braying at full height and at full, flapping wingspan, all of this at the first touch of land,' Conán Maol said.

'A whole night in a cave and, as though it had just invented hearing, the sound of a drop of water falling into a well I too would have fallen into had I kept going,' Oisín said.

'A curlew that has been two months away on her breeding-ground, the first call of that curlew from her home shore in early August,' Goll mac Mórna said.

'The music of Clíodhna's wave washing its broken divinity over my bare feet,' Lughaidh Lagha said.

'And you, Fionn,' Oscar asked, 'what music most pleases you?'

'The music of what happens,' Fionn said.

Let us think about what happens: the last quarter of the moon, a perfect, upright crescent, sinks into the gap between two mountains; in what is only yet an inkling of a breeze an oak growing alone sheds nine acorns, three of them falling out of their cups; his five hinds lying nearby, all the way up from his not yet satisfied sirloin a stag bellows challenge and defiance to all-comers; after three days of rain, where ordinarily there are only three streams, now there are nine streams foaming down the side of a mountain; coming back up above water, a cormorant circles and circles, and furiously circles, seeking to swallow a trout, the trout, out of water, a bundle of spasms; black on a yellow dandelion, a fly cleans his eyes and his wings with his legs; as good as her name, a jaguar turns night to day with her screech; sixty thousand Romans roar their approval of Caligula's thumbs-down disapproval of a new young gladiator from Tunisia; his mouth a Colosseum of anticipated carnage, a mountain lion leaps on a moose calf; sloes on a leafless blackthorn, some of them still in their blue bloom, the others glossy black; walking home along a road that runs by a river a man keeps pace with a heron: an eel in her crop, she labours wide-winged and slow-winged into the wind; finding it, a stoat wreaks fantastic infanticide on a wren's nest; in a canvas currach off the west coast a lone fisherman hauls yet more disappointment, a lobster pot with only a jack crab in it, his great claws snapping at air; in Africa, in the swamplands of the upper Nile, there are older than Cretaceous stirrings in a crocodile's nest of eggs; a shark fin slicing the Pacific reminds us that, even now in our world, there is all too little for conscience to hold on with, all too little for it to hold on to; something we mythically knew we now know scientifically: we know that inwardly, in its very structure, the human hand shakes hands with the shark's fin but, goose quill in hand, there he is, Johann Sebastian Bach scoring our redemption; an old stag and a young challenger crashing antlers; a birch tree in October yellowing sunlight; a whitish, water-soft slug eating a crimson-capped toadstool on the damp, dark floor of a wood; a vixen, her mating call, like her fur, on fire; the difference between a seal struggling down to the sea and that same seal, seconds later, in the sea; how a loud river looks when, walking towards it, we have only yet seen it as sounds; a furze bush growing alone, all its spider webs made visible by mist or dew; mountains so blue, if you didn't know better you'd set out, like a child, to walk through them.

To live in harmony with the music of what happens, even though dreadful things should happen to him, that, without it being a purpose consciously pursued, was Fionn's eventually habitual way.

Wise in the way that the Salmon of Wisdom who lives in Linn Feic in the Boyne is wise, Fionn never wished to remake the world to his liking. It was above all in difficult places, in places out of bounds for very danger, that Fionn could see how soon we would sicken and die out in a world remade to our convenience.

To many people the stuff the universe is made of is something they call matter. To William Blake, nature and presumably, therefore, the universe is Imagination. To Fionn the universe is music.

If the universe is music, if it's subatomic particles are quavers, then it could be argued that it is in being sym-phonic with it that we prosper.

But how, with a good conscience, can I be sym-phonic with tyger when she shrieks, with jaguar when he pounces on his now helpless prey, with cougar when he rips open the belly of a fawn, that preliminary to gorging himself? How, in good conscience, can I be sym-phonic or, yet more seriously, how can I be homeo-phonic with Bear in his Song of Himself? How can I be either sym-phonic or homeo-phonic with Wolf in his howling?

Homeo-phonic with Bear to the point of being a were-bear, with Wolf to the point of being a were-wolf?

In Ireland, at the time that Fionn flourished, Wolf and Bear fought for the crown. First, a man called Art, meaning Bear, had it. Then a man called Lughaidh mac Con, Lughaidh son of Wolf, seized it. Eventually, a man called Cormac mac Airt, Cormac son of Bear, regained it. In this archetypal saga, at once exiguously and immensely significant, it does seem that, whereas Lughaidh was were-wolfish, neither Art nor Cormac mac Airt, his son, was were-bearish. Rather the opposite. Although both bearish and wolfish in nature and nurture, Cormac eventually emerged among us as an Irish Orpheus. During his reign, instead of him being were-bearishly homeophonic with savage nature it was savage nature that was benignly homeophonic with him in his pagan saintliness. Even more famously was this the case during the reign of a later king called Conaire Mór. Walking naked to Tara where he would be crowned king, Con-aire had already inhaled the bonefire smoke of all of his earlier animal incarnations, Wolf and Bear among them.

Twice in Ireland an indigenous Orpheus was high king.

In an old book, Ingcél, a young man, asks Fer Rogain, an old man, about Conaire's reign:

> *'Cid ahé libse a flaithius ind fir sin i tír nÉrenn?' or Ingcél.*
> *'Is maith a flaith,' ol Fer Rogain. 'Ní taudchaid nél tar gréin ó gabais flaith ó medón erraich co medón fogmair, ocus ní taud-chaid banna drúchtae di feór co medón lai, ocus ní fascnan gaemgaeth cairchech cethrae co nónae, ocus ní foruich mac tibhri ina flaith tar ag fireand cacha indise ón chind mbliadnae co araill. Ocus ataat .uii. meic thiri i ngiallnai fri raigid ina thigseom fri coimét in rechtai sin ocus atá cúlaitiri iarna cúl .i. Macc Locc ocus is é taccair tar a cend hi tig Conaire. Is ina flaith is combind la cach fer guth araili ocus betis téta mendchrot ar febus na cána ocus in tsída ocus in chaínchomraic fil sethnu na Hérind. Is ina flaith ataat na trí bairr for Érind .i. barr dés ocus barr scoth ocus barr measa.'*

'What', asked Ingcél, 'are the virtues of his reign in Ireland?'

'A good reign it is,' replied Fer Rogain. 'Since he became king no cloud covers the sun from the middle of spring until the middle of autumn and not a drop of dew evaporates from the grass till midday and no gust of wind shakes a cow's tail till evening and in any one year a wolf will take only one bull calf from an enclosure and in guarantee of this agreement seven wolves remain as hostages by the wall of his house and, by way of further assurance, Mac Locc pleads their case in Conaire's house. To his neighbour each man's voice is as melodious as the strings of harps and that because of the excellence of law and of peace and goodwill that is now to be found throughout Ireland. It is in Conaire's reign that we have the three crowns of Ériu, the crown of corn, the crown of flowers and the crown of acorns.'

Could it be that to have arrived at such a state of grace we must at some stage have been suckled by the animal in us. As an infant, living with his mother in the wilderness, Cormac was stolen and suckled by a milch wolf. But what of animal nature in himself? Was he nourished or suckled by it all his life long? And is that the difference between him and us? Is that the difference between him and the man who shot and killed Ireland's last wolf? How much of what is real in us took its two last lopes, then lurched, and died that night?

Things didn't look good for Cormac early on. What a hybrid he was! What an out and out mongrel he was! Not that he was exceptional in this. We only have to look inside our brains to see how hybrid, how mongrel, we ourselves are. Whereas in Ireland long ago it was Wolf and Bear and Boy who fought for the crown, within us it is Fish and Reptile and Primate and Boy who fight for it. A nursery rhyme that doesn't rhyme we are. Given our enormities in good and evil, in wickedness and saintliness, Blake would have done well to have written one more Song of Experience, six stanzas proceeding to a necessarily more searching question:

Did he who made the Lamb make man?

or

Did he who made Tyger make man?

Compared to us Tyger is splendidly inconsiderable.

What compared to the roaring Colosseum is a roaring lion?

What compared to our Song of Ourselves is Bear's Song of Himself?

Compared to the human baby who so lovingly embraces him, Bear is teddy bear, shuffling about in the wilderness, resorting to occasional atrocities there.

And yet, while by reason of nature and nurture, Cormac might well have become a were-bear or a were-wolf or both together, it was in the end a memorable human being who, without fighting, won the fight for the crown. Remembering him we know that blessedness is possible in the mongrel middle ground between animal and angel.

Back to history made in the Maam Valley.

It wasn't Bear who silenced Céol Cúainc in Ireland. It wasn't Wolf who silenced Bear, the last four lines of his song left unsung:

Where I walk, one to be feared I am
Where I walk, long life
One to be feared I am
There is danger where I walk.

Bear's Song silenced and the language of the megalithic builders, that also silenced. What kind of language was it, this language from before the Indo-European languages? As well as denominating reality was it hospitable to it? Did every verb and noun of it have an aperture and a passage in it? An aperture through which reality could enter and a passage along which it could travel to its own supreme significance in a ritual of death and rebirth?

And we didn't build a Newgrange or a Knowth or a Dowth in which to speak the last remembered words of what, very likely, was a big way of seeing and knowing the world. The megalithic way of seeing it and knowing it.

Megalithic language, or languages, we silenced; Bear language we silenced; Boar language we silenced; Wolf language we silenced.

Our history is the history of our success in making ourselves and our world unreal.

Mostly, it is from unreality that we suffer. From that, and from the wrong kind of man-made reality.

What remains to us is Bear's bed in Aillwee Cave.

Recognizing our plight, and therefore vicariously for us all, maybe someone will someday go back to it, will lie in it, will fall asleep in it, will dream in it. In that dream, we will know that the whole Cormac-mac-Airt-Cormac-mac-Con adventure into a blessed humanity is enacting itself in us all over again.

What it comes down to is a choice between being unreal in an unreal world and being real in a real world.

Sadly, we haven't yet seen that prospering man-made unreality is, if anything, more dangerous to us than prospering, primal reality was.

Better Céol Cúaine than the ever-hungering, ever-unhappy, ever-unsatisfied, inaudibly howling vacancy we have replaced it with.

Walk the land now and again and again and again we walk into such vampiring vacancies.

Better any day our chances with a real wolf than with the Wolf of Vacancy.

In Nordic myth this Wolf of Vacancy is called Fenris Wolf or, as commonly, Fenrir. In order for our world to be at all possible, so the story goes, Tyr, a great and mighty god, had to bind him, had to lay him up in chains in an underworld. But everyone, including Tyr himself, knows full well that Fenrir will one day slip his chains, he will emerge and run free. Opening his mouth, he will advance his lower jaw under the earth and his upper jaw over the sun. Sun and earth and all in between he will swallow, and for Fenrir that is just a first mouthful.

Ever since we first set foot in Ireland we have been creating our own Fenrir, our own Wolf of Vacancy, our own Apocalyptic Wolf of Apocalyptic Vacancy.

What we would see if we lifted our eyes from our ledgers is that at this stage there is no binding him, no laying him up in chains, out of sight, in an underworld.

So here it is, *Foras Feasa ar Éirinn*:

Lights gone out in Ireland's last wolf are lights coming on
in a not inconsiderably larger wolf,
are lights coming on
in
The Wolf of Vacancy.

Amhairghin's Fourteenth I Am: His Tragodia, His Goatsong

I HAD often heard it said that you can take the man from the bog but you can't take the bog from the man. I was myself within three weeks of being ordained a priest and within three months of taking up a lectureship in Classics when, without warning, the bog won. That didn't mean that I had bartered the Gospels for the Satyr play. What I told myself was that I must refuse definition. Not just definition by Christian collar and academic gown. All definition conferred or imposed by society, in splendid array, saying yes to itself. It all went back to a morning when I was fifteen. With our two sheep dogs, my father and my uncle and myself set off for the mountains and by three o'clock that day, the dogs having backed him into a shallow shaft at the base of a cliff, we had him, his horns flowing grandly back and up and out behind his withers, his beard flowing down below his knees, his nostrils so pretty I was ashamed of my own nose, his hooves so trim and so delicate that, certainly up here in these, his heights, I felt awkward and flatfooted. But that of course wasn't all. There was a smell off him that would almost knock you, and by that alone we knew that we had found what we had climbed for, the bravest and grandest and most majestic wild goat of them all, and that evening, railed in at the top of a

scaffold half as high as our high church, he was the newly inaugurated, crowned king of our town and king of the three-day
fair, called Puck Fair, in his honour.

As I came out of a shop next day the sun came out from
behind a thunder cloud and the shadow of the goat fell full
upon me, so that for a dreadful instant his beard was my beard,
his horns my horns, his hooves my hooves. Unarguably, the
thing coming down upon me, unarguably for that moment, it
was a destiny.

I fled from it, for as I saw things in those days, I couldn't be
both Christian and who I was. It was only at the expense of who
I was that I could be a Christian.

Harshly, at the expense of who I was, that's how I lived for
the next nine years.

Listening to them morning, noon and evening, and thinking of them as heavenly hammer blows, I would lay myself
open, as open as hot horse-shoe iron on an anvil, to all eighteen
strokes of the Angelus, three followed by three followed by three
then followed by nine in slow but determined succession, and
that I would do in the hope that I might one day look up, on
Judgment Day look up, and find myself acceptable in God's
eyes.

Three weeks short of consecration, without warning one
night, I lost the fight. I came home, and in August on all three
days of Puck, on gathering day, middle day and scattering day,
I held my own with neighbours and strangers who came over to
drink with me, not one of us so much as lifting his glass above
the common secret, so well kept from ourselves, that we were
drinking to the high good health of His Majesty crowned with
rings and strings of mountain flowers about and upon his horns,
and in its way that was a blessing because, so unlike early Greece
in this, our myths were much too polite to sponsor what it was
we were doing, they were much too polite to bring what it was
we were doing out into the open.

It took me all of thirty years to come to terms with what
happened to me in the sweet-shop doorway, and I only came to

terms with it then because I saw it and welcomed it as a Christian destiny, pioneered and therefore sponsored by Jesus in Gethsemane. Instead of driving them underground, I attempted to live my instincts, from their darkest roots up I attempted to live them, into sanctity. I lost that fight too of course, but instead of giving up didn't I one day stand unredeemed before God, and in some ways it worked.

By the time I was safe to live with and was again respectable, I was too old to get married.

So you have me now. Jimmy Lyne is my name. I live alone at the foot of the Reeks. I go to Mass every Sunday. And every year, come August, I go to Puck Fair, our festival, in our town, of being honest with ourselves and with God.

Changed Utterly

SCENE: THE HAWK'S WELL

MORE SHADE than image in his Dreaming Back, Yeats climbs to the Hawk's Well. More image than shade, Maud Gonne is sitting beside it. Courtesy prevailing over sudden, unaccountable bashfulness, he sits opposite her.

MG: By your boots and trousers legs I see how overgrown with heather and bracken and briars is the path to wonder.

WB: A wonder it is, this well. It is on a hill high above the sea. Hard, and of unfissured gneiss, the Ox Mountains lie between it and the sea. And yet, night and day, no moon or full moon, it ebbs and flows with the tide. And what is more, its water is sometimes salt, sometimes sweet.

MG: What a wonder it is, this small well! What a wonder it is in its dilapidated ordinariness!

WB: And the wonder of it by credulous consent, the wonder of its ebbing and flowing, what of that?

MG: It isn't why I am here. I am here to learn ordinariness. Ordinary water mirroring an ordinary sky.

WB: And the hawk? What if it suddenly mirrored the hawk?

MG: The hawk is your invention.

WB: Not my invention. In a dream one night I cupped my hand down into it. So nearly dead from thirst was I, I ignored

114

the outraged screech of a hawk above me. Half way to my mouth, my fingers withered into hawk talons and the water fell back.

MG: Then what?

WB: My thirst getting the better of me, I tried again.

MG: And then?

WB: A third time the same thing, only worse. This time I couldn't shake the hawk talons back into a human hand.

MG: But you did, eventually. How?

WB: It's a long story.

MG: Too long for the telling?

WB: There is more to the world than meets the modern eye or the modern mind. It is to seek healing from that eye and mind that I am here, at the Hawk's Well, called that for a reason hanging now above us in the air, hanging now beneath us in the well.

And so, as for the ordinariness you would learn, cup your pearl-pale, Cathleen Ni Houlihan hand down into it, bring it to your mouth and see what will happen.

MG: The hawk throwing his thunder on the stones?

WB: Things being what they are, we should always be ready for something alarmingly more in them than the utmost that we can empirically know of them, and it was this something more, ordinarily reserved, that screeched above me in my dream. Not only above me, of course. The hawk of the Hawk's Well has screeched above an entire people.

MG: Meaning that things are fighting back against our modern way of perceiving them?

WB: Meaning just that.

MG: Meaning that Cú Chulainn, the national hero, must come all the way back from revolutionary politics in the General Post Office, must come back to this, the Hawk's Well.

WB: Revolutions in politics are effective essentially not just circumstantially when they have their original and continuing source in our prior re-education at the well.

MG: Cú Chulainn cupping his hand down into the something more in things – in that our re-instauration as a people!

WB: The Fifth Province more a deed than a place. A deed not a place. My mistake was that I staged him more or less as I found him, a defender not an innovator.

MG: You had him fight the invulnerable tide. Now he must sit by a well that ebbs and flows with the tide, even if it does so only in popular credulity.

WB: Given how the world is, science is as much a liability as superstition used to be. I agree with you, though. It is only because we are used to them that ordinary things aren't as insurgently numinous to us as they actually are.

MG: But the tall tales that give life to Cú Chulainn, are they not as topplingly tall as they are for the reason that they are addicted to the outlandish?

WB: All land, even tired farmland, is outlandish. It is insurgent alike to the securities of science and superstition. It is insurgent alike to idle and exact sensation. It is what this well in its dilapidated ordinariness is saying to you, isn't it?

MG: So why the hawk? Mirrored in it, hovering in it, the hawk is a distraction.

WB: Reality fell out of the hand with which I would have apprehended it. So with my eyes. So with my mind.

So with John Locke's philosophy.

Cup John Locke's philosophy down into this well and see what happens as you draw it up to your mouth. Cup $E = mc^2$ down into it and see what will happen.

Whether with hand or eye or mind, it is in apprehending things that we lose things.

Whether with hand or eye or mind, we shouldn't therefore be apprehensive of things.

It is with an eye not apprehensive that we see things as they are.

It is with a hand not apprehensive that we bring clear clarifying water to our mouths.

Evict apprehensiveness from your hand and reality will be to hand.

It is apprehensiveness that degrades seeing into sight.

MG: Are your saying that it was the apprehensiveness of a raptor's talons that you shook out of your hands, that you shook out of your eyes?

WB: The apprehending hawk's foot in hearing, seeing, touch, taste, smell, in instinct and intellect, that is what was shown to me in my dream.

What I learned is that where satori naturally is; sight apprehensively is.

Sight is usurpation. Endlessly frustrated usurpation. As I've said, in seeking to close its ocular talons on reality it spills reality.

MG: You are seeking, aren't you, to enlist me in an Easter insurrection against ourselves?

WB: This time also we will call on Cú Chulainn our national hero, but only for the reason that he too must fight the hawk's foot in his hand. In the national hand.

MG: History you are saying has come to the Hawk's Well?

WB: To the screech of a kestrel, not, as I used to think, to the scream of Juno's peacock.

MG: Given the choice, would you reincarnate within hearing of a Zen gong in Kyoto or within hearing of a Christian gong in Byzantium?

WB: Given the choice, I'd be born out of wedlock to a girl in that white house, the nearest one there, under this hill. That way, within hearing of the screech, I'd be less likely to waste my time cupping John Locke's philosophy down into the well. That way I wouldn't waste my time cupping $E = mc^2$ down into it.

MG: Have you given up on eye and mind?

WB: What I know now and what I hope I will anamnesially know in my next incarnation is that the hawk is forever too wild to come down and sit on my wrist.

Here at the Hawk's Well is my Easter Rising against the hawk's talons in my hand.

MG: The apprehensive hand with which you cannot bring immortal water to your mouth. The apprehensive hand with which you wrote *Cathleen Ni Houlihan.*

WB: As I see her now, she voyages with Máel Dúin.

MG: From where to where?

WB: From an island we can to an island we cannot lay claim to.

MG: To where we are?

WB: A land beyond anything heart or mind can desire, or hand can apprehend.

Shaman

BEING AWAKE in the way that modern people are awake isn't something I'm good at. After only a few years in it, therefore, I left the modern world and came back, putting my hand, happily now, to the spade and the shovel I had left down.

Ivy I had planted against the walls had grown thick and strong, blinding two windows. I didn't cut it, preferring an intuitive twilight in the house. It was for the same reason also that I didn't often light the lamp. Even on winter nights I didn't often light it. Itself so full of shadows, there is more understanding in firelight for the kind of man I am.

Bringing water from the well and the turf from the shed, these were the last two jobs I would do, darkness closing in, on a winter's evening.

If the weather was hard I'd select hard sods. Cut from the deepest spit of a high bog, they were older, I'd remind myself sometimes, than Ireland's oldest folktale.

What that folktale was I didn't know, but how strange it was, crossing a yard at nightfall with a prehistoric landscape in a bag on my back. For the rest of the night I would sit prehistorically by the fire and life and light of it. That suited me. That was something I was good at. It came naturally to me on winter nights to sink to the sod's level. It came naturally to me, sitting there, to sink into the deepest spit of mind in me. And that was a dreaming spit, dreaming its dream with a hawthorn bush, dreaming their dreams with mountain and star.

One night the chimney wasn't drawing so well. The wind was from the north and when it gusted there would be a down-draught of billowing, blue smoke into the room.

It was hard on my eyes. I closed them, continuing to sit there, inhaling the fragrance.

Soon something was happening. Landscapes I had glimpses of, landscapes Partholon might have walked in, were taking me over. It was like they were fostering me. I was and yet I wasn't myself. I was their dream of me. I was doing their dream of me. I was digging peat. In the deepest spit, between two tree stumps, I uncovered a pair of boots. Of deerhide I thought. But I could-n't be sure, so strangely transparent in places were they. Going up onto the bank, I put off my own boots and I put them on, criss-crossing a tracery of thongs about my shins and collops, knotting them under my knees. To test them, to get the feel of them, I got up and started walking, going the wind's way.

A lake I came to, following an otter path, was strange. It didn't mirror some things it should mirror. It didn't mirror a red horse on a ridge. It didn't mirror its own islands. It didn't mir-ror a wood growing along one side of it. And yet, so clear, so deadly calm, so far-sighted a lake I had never seen. It mirrored mountains so far away it must, you would think, be clairvoyant.

Otters, I thought, wouldn't lead me astray, wouldn't lead me to evil, so I kept to the path, going with it, not frightened.

As I entered the wood the horse on the ridge behind me neighed. It was a red neighing.

Farther along I smelled something dead. Something big, I thought, a boar or a deer. And though I searched a long while, I found no carcass. There was no sign of carnivorous feeding.

How can this be? I wondered, walking on. How can there be such a strong smell of death where nothing has died.

From a long way off I heard it. It was a birch. Invisible beings wielding invisible axes were felling it. It was frightful. Every axe blow to it was an axe blow to me. All savage damage to it was savage damage to me. I was a limbless trunk. Infinitely felled, infinitely hurt, I was a stump of me.

I was me and I kept going.

The two sides of the path came together. I entered thick darkness and I didn't see the house until, seeing an old man by the fire, I realized I'd already walked into it.

The chair he pointed to was withered. He was withered himself. And the fire was withered.

It was a fire of three last gasps. It gave no heat. But it didn't go out.

The house smelled of stored apples, like apples in March, too shrivelled for use.

'Where am I?' I asked.

What where could there be when the two sides of your path have come together? What where could there be when both sides of the mirror are blind?

Even his words were withered. Leaving his mouth they were withered. They were born withered.

'Only people the lake doesn't mirror come this far,' he said.

I kept silent, wondering.

'I knew you were coming,' he said. 'I heard the red neighing.'

'Where are we?' I asked.

'In a wood,' he said.

'What wood? Where?'

'In a wood between worlds, which the lake doesn't mirror.'

'Does it mirror this house?'

'No.'

'Does it mirror the smoke from its chimney?'

'There is no smoke from its chimney.'

'Does it mirror you?'

He didn't answer.

'Does it mirror me?'

'No, it doesn't mirror you. You heard the red neighing, didn't you? And there's something more. It was your own death, all your own deaths, that you smelled coming into the wood.'

'Who are you?' I asked.

'I'm the mask of your own state of mind. As you yourself are so do you see me.'

'You have otter's whiskers.'

'Have I?'

'An otter path led to your house.'

'If it did, then it led to that,' he said, pointing to a hag-bed I hadn't seen. I went and lay down.

'And now,' he said, bending over me, touching my mouth with his stick, 'now you must ask no more questions. Your words have no meanings now. Like the boughs outside all their meanings have fallen from them. All their mirrorings are quenched.'

I felt weak.

So weak I couldn't even be weak.

Consciousness blurred. It brightened. It blurred. Breathing was hard. Every breath was the last breath, the death-rattle breath, of beings I had been. In a seizure of sightless seeing I had unblurred, perfect vision of a doe I had been. All my deaths were dying me now. Like the fire, it wasn't for life, it was for death I was gasping. Only all my deaths were life in me, and it death-rattled me, and it death-rattled me, and it death-rattled me, and then, in a moment of clarity, consenting to be, consenting not to be, it death-rattled the life I'd been living, modern life, out of me. And now, when I thought it was over, it came again death-rattling six spit of history out of me.

Like a dropped fawn, mother-licked, I struggled to my feet. But there was no chair, no fire.

Like a mirror turned away, there was no house.

Self-detached, like placenta, and fallen to the ground, the boots I'd been wearing were being overgrown. Looking at them, I felt sure that in time a high bog would cover them.

The boots I had put off I found, how, I don't know. And I came home, how I don't know. I only know that I was sitting in my own chair by my own fire when I heard a knocking.

The man who opened my door and came in had come, he said, because he had dreamed that I was a healer.

Epilogue

So, YES, Orpheus in Ireland is a struggle. It isn't only that the boar turned on us. It is when and where he turned on us, turning love to licbestod in an all too murderous way. Also, it is whence he turned on us, from within, charging us as we lay in the unsafe lair of each other's embrace. Far worse than we feared, it was havoc. And now, unsure of ourselves, we looked back to a time when the island was Iath nAnann, the land of the goddess Danu and her people, their music, heard in out of the way places, the chief reason why we aren't as ignorant and brutal as we might be, Fomorians, cormorant-tongued.

Ireland is a land of three dimensions, Banbha, Fódhla and Éire. Unfortunately for the goddess who has given her name to it, Éire is now the overt, official dimension, a place you would be ashamed of when you look away from it and look at a tree. Not a single building that you could compare your love to in the way that you would compare her, in her breasts compare her, to two young roes. And how long since Fír Flathemon, the ontological sovereignty of a ruler that sustains his institutional sovereignty, made a king's reign radiant in both justice and truth? How long since Blocc and Bluigne, the two druidic standing stones, opened before us, letting us through to a momentary but, in effect, enduring vision of how unworldly the world is? How long since Fál, the stone phallus, screeched its acceptance of us, recognizing our right to occupy the land, a right depending on our willingness and ability to live symphonically and sympathetically with all things? Sympathetically with the land we plough, with the tree we cut down. That surely is why Conaire reached out his hand for the hurt bird to perch on. That is why he accepted the hurt. That is why the Birdreign: a reign ecumenical across all that exists.

Coming forward to Christian times: it is in his choice of himself, not because nature in him is different from ours, that Ciarán of Saighir is exceptional.

Essentially, to talk about dimensions of Ireland is to talk about modes and moods of seeing. Seek for Fódhla not on horseback riding northwards, not in a boat sailing westwards. Seek her in seeing. Some days I walk out my own door and I find myself walking in an undamageable dimension of the universe. The change I soon realize isn't in things, it is in me a perceiver of things. I can call the change Banbha, I can call it Fódhla, and for as long as I am out there seeing things as I do I live in the dimension of Ireland called Fódhla. If I met him coming towards me along the path I'd know I had something uncommon in common with Ollamh Fódhla.

This change I am talking about, Dylan Thomas called it 'Fern Hill':

> And nightly under the simple stars
> As I rode to sleep the owls were bearing the farm away,
> All the moon long I heard, blessed among stables, the
>   nightjars
>   Flying with the ricks and the horses
>   Flashing into the dark.
>
> And then to awake, and the farm, like a wanderer white
> With the dew, come back, the cock on his shoulder: it was all
>   Shining, it was Adam and maiden,
>   The sky gathered again
>   And the sun grew round that very day,
> So it must have been after the birth of the simple light
> In the first spinning place, the spellbound horses walking
>   warm

Out of the whinnying green stable
On to the fields of praise.

Celts had to wait a long time for their own account of the
birth of the universe but, re-emerging with Dylan from the pre-
cosmic dark, our daytime consciousness gathers again, we open
our eyes and we know, in lauds we know, that it was worth waiting for.

In Fern Hill sleep we travel back to the first morning of the
world or, as a philosophical idealist might have it, in Fern Hill
sleep we travel back to paradisal perception.

Either way, the question remains: how, without violating it,
do we plough a field of praise? With a plough that is praise? The
ploughman praise? All of it lauds?

As if he too had travelled to it in Fern Hill sleep, Edwin
Muir awakened one day to vision:

Those lumbering horses in the steady plough,
On the bare field – I wonder why, just now,
They seemed terrible, so wild and strange,
Like magic power on the stony grange.

Perhaps some childish hour has come again,
When I watched fearful, through the blackening rain,
Their hooves like pistons in an ancient mill
Move up and down, yet seem like standing still.

Their conquering hooves which trod the stubble down
Were ritual that turned the field to brown,
And their great hulks were seraphim of gold,
Or mute ecstatic monsters on the mould.

And oh the rapture, when, one furrow done,
They marched broad-breasted to the sinking sun!
The light flowed off their bossy sides in flakes;
The furrows rolled behind like struggling snakes.

But when at dusk with steaming nostrils home
They came, they seemed gigantic in the gloom,

And warm and glowing with mysterious fire
That lit their smouldering bodies in the mire.

Their eyes as brilliant and as wide as night
Gleamed with a cruel apocalyptic light.
Their manes the leaping ire of the wind
Lifted with rage invisible and blind.

Ah, now it fades! it fades! And I must pine
Again for that dread country crystalline,
Where the blank field and the still-standing tree
Were bright and fearful presences to me.

As in the Orkneys so in Ireland.

In Ireland also, Orpheus is seeing as well as hearing.

How do you buy and sell those apocalyptic horses?

How do you buy and sell the first morning of the world?

How do you say of a field of praise that it is property, my property?

How, sailing up Kenmare Bay, do you take possession of Iath nAnann?

How do you take possession of a dimension of Ireland called Fódhla?

It is the question Yeats and Maud Gonne are struggling with at the Hawk's Well.

Either with your eyes or with your hands, you don't apprehend Paradise. You don't take it to hand, close your fist on it, and say, it is mine. That way we lose it. That way we lost it.

Our Fall, to begin with, was a fall into apprehensive seeing.
It is apprehension in seeing that blinds seeing.
Apprehension in seeing is the eclipse of seeing.

Momentarily in Edwin Muir the eclipse evanesced and there they were:

Their eyes as brilliant and as wide as night

And they gleamed, those eyes,

Gleamed with a cruel apocalyptic light.

Cruel in themselves and cruel to us who would buy them and sell them, who would seek to own them, listing them as ours in our Domesday Book.

Think of the Aillwee Bear. Think of him singing his Song of Himself:

There is danger where I move my feet
I am whirlwind
There is danger where I move my feet
I am a grey bear
When I walk, where I step, lightning flies from me
Where I walk, one to be feared I am
Where I walk, long life
One to be feared I am
There is danger where I walk.

Shouldn't someone sing that song in Aillwee Cave?

Shouldn't someone walk the land singing that song?

As Yeats and Maud Gonne did, shouldn't we go back to the Hawk's Well and let the apprehending raptor's talons that are in them fall out of our hands and eyes.

It will be a long, shamanic journey back.

A journey through the bonefire of the bones of all our incarnations.

Amhairghin Glúngheal journeying back through the stag bones, the hawk bones, the boar bones, the salmon bones of who he simultaneously is.

A big journey it is, this journey back through all the last breaths, the death-rattling last breaths of beings I have been:

Consciousness blurred. It brightened. It blurred. Breathing was hard. Every breath was the last breath, the death-rattle breath, of beings I had been. In a seizure of sightless seeing I had unblurred, perfect vision of a doe I had been. All my deaths were dying me now. Like the fire, it wasn't for life, it was for death I was gasping. Only all my deaths were life in me, and it death-rattled me, and it death-rattled me, and it death-rattled me, and then, in a moment of clarity, consenting to be, consenting not to be, it death-rattled the life I'd been living, modern life, out of me. And now, when I thought it was over, it came again death-rattling six spit of history out of me.

Ecumenical across all elements and all species, Amhairghin can now set his unapprehending right foot on a shingle shore in Ireland, for that is what Banbha means.

Unlike everything that Éire has come to mean, Banbha means not apprehending, either with our hands or with our eyes.

My house is mirrored in Linn Feic.

In a sense therefore I sleep in Linn Feic, I dream in Linn Feic.

At a sleeping depth of me that I'm not aware of, maybe I am a salmon in Linn Feic, and maybe I swim upstream every night, all the way up into the Otherworld, all the way up into Connla's Well. At that depth of myself, maybe the shadows of the Otherworld hazel are always upon me. Are always upon all of us, letting wisdom and wonder drop down into us.

That is everyone's ninth 'I am', Am hé i llind, I am a salmon in a pool, and every salmon in every pool is the divine salmon in Linn Feic. Sadly, for all his searching in what he called the id, Freud didn't come upon that divine salmon nor is there evidence that he ever remembered his nights in the well, well below the id, under the hazel.

Having gone below all that is phylogenetic in us, having gone below the well and the hazel in us, Ollamh Fódhla can surely say what the sage of the Chandogya Upanishad says, 'tat tvam asi', that thou art. And where, we wonder, does that leave Amhairghin Glúngheal, he still singing his song of who he elementally, phylogenetically and gnostically is? Not sage enough, even if he does so to Orphic intent and effect, to sing us ashore?

It would be wise to settle for something a long way short of perfection.

Knowing from experience what folktales know, Fintan mac Bochra tells us that being human is a habit that can be broken. In what he says, Ollamh Fódhla implies that being human is a habit we can nightly break and nightly reassume.

For all that seems to be so incorrigible in us we are possibility more than we are fatality. And that is true also of nature as a whole. Else no evolution. Else no trilobite. Else no swallow. His fierce intent notwithstanding, the hawk, our fifth 'I am', cannot ensure that things will continue convenient to his hooked head and hooked feet. In him somewhere unknown to him the hawk can ascend as surely as can the salmon into the well overarched by the hazel. And, after 'tat tvam asi', that is the next most marvellous statement that we can make about the universe.

It is good, in our talk about the universe, that we aren't as cormorant-tongued as we might be.

It is good, in our dealings with the universe, that our hands aren't fully what they might be, crab claws opening and closing apprehensively upon it.

Am hé i llind
I am a salmon in a pool

To ascend into Ireland is to ascend under the hazel that overarches our seeing, that overarches our knowing, that overarches our doing.

Everyone an Amhairghin Glúngheal in this adventure, we must do what he did, only not as he did it. Coming in through the nine waves, each wave an initiation into wonder, we must set our right foot on a shingle shore in Kenmare Bay.

Knowing that foot to be an evolved fin, we will do well if, instead of boastfully singing Amhairghin's thirteen 'I ams', we Orphically sing a single 'I am'.

Am Énflaith

It is what Fintan mac Bochra was. It is what Ciarán of Saighir was, it is what Cormac mac Airt was, it is what Conaire Mór was.

We remember that on his way to Tara, there to inherit his royalty, Conaire had to walk through the bonefire of all his previous 'I ams'. Inhaling the smoke of them and in that way reinheriting them, he became single and could say

Conaire I am

Instead of being an adjunct, ego is now a centre of total coherence, all that we have been and are radiating out from it in perfect presence to itself and to all things. That is royalty of achieved being, not royalty by coronation. This, in part, is what enabled Ogma to go into the heart of Fomorian darkness and bring home its stolen soul to Ireland. Failure in this was tragic for Diarmaid and, at one remove, for Gráinne. Contrarywise, failure in this led to the death of Ireland's last wolf.

We have been seeking to imagine and enact an Orphic ascent into Ireland. That as distinct from our repeated and continuing attempts to take possession of it by force of arms. Almost all of what Ireland is we lose in our efforts to conquer it and hold it militarily. The one an eschatological image, the other an eschatological shade, that is what Yeats and Maud Gonne are discovering at the Hawk's Well. Oddly, it is because of the clutching hawk talons in our hands that we cannot bring the world-mirroring water to our mouths. The Ireland that is worth living in is the Ireland that cannot be clutched, either by John Bull or by Cathleen Ni Houlihan.

Gesang ist Dasein
Dasein ist Gesang

Amhairghin's three songs we have. They are different songs altogether, and they work wonders, not least upon ourselves, when we sing them Orphically.

And that, to the sound of shore shingle under our feet, is what we do now:

Am gaeth i mmuir
Am tond trethan
Am fuaim mara

Am dam secht ndrenn
Am séig i n-aill
Am dér gréne
Am cáin
Am torc ar gail
Am hé i llind
Am loch i mmaig
Am brí dánae
Am gaí i fodb feras fechtu
Am dé delbas do chind codnu

Cóich é nod gleith clochor slébe?
Cia ón cotagair aesa éscai?
Cia dú i llaig funiud gréne?
Cia bier buar ó thigh Temrach?
Cia buar Tethrach tibde?
Cia dain, cia dé, delbas faebru?
Andind; ailsiu cáinte im gaí, cáinte gaithe.

Iascach muir
Mothach tir
Tomaidm n-eisc
Iasca and
Fo thuind en
Lethach mil
Partach lag
Tomaidm n-eisc
Iascach muir.

Ailiu iath n-hErend
Hermach hermach muir
Mothach mothach sliab
Srathach srathach caill
Cithach cithach aub
Essach essach loch.

Songs that bring a hollow handful of world-mirroring water to
our mouths.

Part II

Manannán in Ireland

Preface

In the person of Moses, the Israelites met God and that meeting became an event in their history.

In the person of Bran mac Feabhail we met God, but that meeting didn't become an event in our history.

Could it be that we can take it into our history now?

In the hope that we can, I will tell the story, twice.

I

Ireland's Bhagavad Gita as a Pagan Might Be Happy to Sing It

GREAT and renowned warrior that he was, it wasn't something that Bran mac Feabhail had ever done, but one day,
drawn to he didn't know what, he walked out of his fortress,
down and away into the wet, wild lands where only snipe and
herons and otters lived. Before long, having always been a man
among men, the silence and the solitude were getting to him. A
red onslaught between mountains, that he could deal with, but
this silence that you couldn't spear, this solitude that you could-
n't bring a sword down upon, even the mist that came down, it
all unnerved him. Suffering his first defeat, he turned for home.
Soon, his walking a trudging, he heard music not of our world
behind him. Turning round, he saw a silver branch. It was out
of it the music came. Strangest of all, the branch didn't play it.
What he heard was the branch being itself. Being itself, it had
perils for mortals in it. And it raided him. In the way that he
himself would raid a triple-ditched ringfort, it raided him. It
raided him, not with spear and torch and sword, but with its
unearthly sweetness it raided him. Almost, almost to swooning.
Then it ceased, and, by the time he came back to himself and
opened his eyes, was gone.

In his hall that night, amidst all the usual goings on, Bran
sat silent and alone.

A hard man in battle and in all his dealings with the world, it had never occurred to him that anything either in the world or from beyond it could have so disabled him.

Whatever else, the music had damaged him in his sense of himself.

And his people – when they came to know, it would damage him in their eyes.

He imagined their great concern. Bran mac Feabhail, the hard man, not foremost in battle. Bran mac Feabhail, his eyes and his mind not fixed on what he was doing. Bran mac Feabhail laid low not by a sword stroke but by longing.

Sensing a sudden silence in the house, he opened his eyes and there she was, a radiant woman, cruel if she needed to be.

Fifty quatrains she sang, singing of the wonders of the land she came from. And he, Bran, him she invited to come to that land. Next morning, in three ships, in each a company of three times nine men, he was on the sea, sailing westward.

After two days and two nights of tough, untoward going, suddenly, instead of sea salt in their eyes and minds, the fragrances, blent and separate, of summer meadows, and there he was, Manannán mac Lir, god of the sea, riding towards them in his four-horse chariot. Singing them out over the manes and heads of his horses, they still trampling, thirty quatrains he sang:

> *Cáini amra laisin mBran*
> *ina churchán tar muir nglan;*
> > *os mé, am charput do chéin,*
> > *is magh sccothach ima-réidh.*
>
> *A n-us muir glan*
> *don náoi broindig a tá Bran,*
> > *is Mag Meall co n-iumat scoth*
> > *damsa a carput dá roth.*
>
> *At-chí Bran*
> *lín tonn tibri tar muir nglan.*
> > *At-chíu ca-déin i mMagh Mon*
> > *sgotha cennderga gin on.*

Taithnit gabra lir a sam
sella roiscc ro sire Bran.
　　　Brundit sscotha sruaim do mil
　　　a crích Manannáin mic Lir.

Lí na fairge fora taí,
geldod mora imme-roí:
　　　ra sert buidhe ocus glas;
　　　is talam nád écomrass.

Lingit ích bricc ass de brú
a muir finn forn-aiccisiu;
　　　it láoig it úain co ndath,
　　　co cairde, cin imarbad.

Cé at-chetha áonchairptheach
i mMag Meall co n-immat scoth,
　　　fil mor di echaib ar brú
　　　cen suide, nát aiccisiu

The god telling us how different is the world as he sees it from the world as we see it.

The god telling us that what we, rising and falling in it, see as grey, salt sea, he sees as a Plain of Delights over which, even now, he is riding in his four-horse chariot.

The god telling us that, if only we had eyes to see, we would see that the silver-branch being itself is no more wonderful than any ordinary ash branch or oak branch being itself.

And what the god doesn't tell us in words he tells us in his singing. His singing being the singing of the silver branch, he tells us that, had we eyes to see it, any ordinary bush being itself would put an end to us being our everyday selves.

Signalling to his men to turn their boats round, Bran sailed home to the land he had left, the land to which the radiant lady had invited him. Waiting for him there on the shore, the silver branch sang the song of his ascent into Ireland.

Over months and then over years it would happen. Bran would be out on his own in the wetlands or he'd be on his way home, alone, from an assembly of his people and, full in front of him on an otter trail or on a chariot road, there it would be, the silver branch singing six other stanzas that Manannán sang at sea:

> *Sech is Manannán mac Lir*
> *asin charput cruth in fir,*
> > *bied dia chlaind densa ngair*
> > *fer cáoin hi curp criad adgil.*

> *Con-lee Manannán mac Lir*
> *luth lighe la Caointigirn:*
> > *gerthair dia mach i mbith gnó;*
> > *ad-ndidma Fiachna mac ndó.*

> *Moidfid sognáis gach sídhe;*
> *bid treitil cach daghthíre;*
> > *at-fii rúna rith ecne*
> > *isin mbith can a ecli.*

> *Bieid hi fethol cech míl*
> *itir glasmuir ocus tír;*
> > *bid druac re mbuidnib hi froiss;*
> > *bid cú allaid cech indroiss.*

> *Bid damh co mbennuiph argait*
> *hi mruig i nd-agthar carpait;*
> > *bid écni brec, i llinn lain;*
> > *bid rón, bid eala fionnbán.*

> *Biaid tre bitha síora*
> *cét mbliadna hi findrighe;*
> > *silis learca lecht imchían;*
> > *dergfaid roí roth imrían.*

Manannán, god of the sea, telling us at sea, or what to us is sea, that he will come ashore into Ireland, that he will lie with a woman called Caointigirn, that a son she and her husband will call Mongán mac Fiachna will be born to her, that he will be welcome in all worlds, that he will be both seer and sage, that sometimes when he talks it will seem like it is the oldest bush in

Ireland that is talking. Other times, listening to him, it will seem like you are surrounded by an oakwood and that it is telling you the deepest common secret of its being and your own being. Perfectly human when he is human, he will not nonetheless be so perfectly held as so many of us are to the habit of being human. When he needs to, he will be a dragon. Not content to know the world in only a human way, he will be seal, he will be swan. Challenging us in our miserable habits of seeing and knowing, he will walk towards us as a silver-antlered stag. A king in the land, he will put down evil but in doing so he will not himself become evil.

Even people who know him only by hearsay will know, hearing about him, that Mongán mac Fiachna is a son of God.

Son of the most tremendous of gods, Manannán mac Lir, god of the sea, of what to us is sea, of what to him is a Plain of Delights.

Never are we so challenged in all that we are as we are when we encounter Manannán.

The instant we meet him we know that eye and mind are habits of eye and mind.

The instant we meet him we know that the world we have lived in was all along but a habit of seeing, a habit of knowing.

The instant we meet him we know that being human is a habit and, walking away, we know how shaken in that habit we now are.

And how glad we are to be so shaken in this habit of being human, shaken in it and, at times, shaken altogether out of it.

To be human, when being human is a habit we have broken, that is a wonder.

And when, as will happen, we take being human for granted, how good it then is to walk out of it and be a seal in the sea off Tory or a swan on Loch Deirg Deirc.

But, having been out of our humanity for days or months or years, there is no wonder so great as the wonder of coming back into it.

The outlandish danger and difficulty of it, that is the wonder of coming back into it, of being in it.

No wonder we so yearningly call upon it to come and condense all about us.

What a wonder and a blessing it is to a naked spirit when a human body begins to condense all about it, when human hearing, seeing, touch, taste and smell condense all about it, when human seeking and knowing condense all about it. Here it is, again setting out on the most perilous of adventures, the adventure of being what we are, human beings for whom our humanity is a conscious choice.

All of this was Bran mac Feabhail's answering song to the Song of God he heard at sea.

Calling for silence, he sang it in his house.

Calling for silence, he sang it at assemblies of his people.

Calling for silence, he sang it at fairs all over the country. Not needing to call for silence, he sang it to otters and herons and snipe in the wetlands.

This was Bran preparing Ireland for the day when Manannán would come ashore into Ireland.

'It's what Ireland means,' Bran one day said to his druid.

'What', his druid asked, 'does Ireland mean?'

'It means what Manannán singing at sea means.'

'Simply it means

Silver-branch perception of things in their silver-branch being.'

'Then Ireland isn't for living in,' the druid said.

'How so?' Bran asked.

'How if I see it in its silver-branch being, how if I hear it in its silver-branch singing in root and branch, can I cut down a tree and make a chariot of it? How if I see it in its silver-branch being, how if I hear it in its silver-branch lowing, can I kill a yearling calf and eat it?'

'A calf out at grass is silver-branch being,' Bran said. 'A calf slaughtered outside in our yard is silver-branch being, is silver-branch singing, in hoof and horn. A beef hanging from a cross beam here in our house is silver-branch being, is silver-branch singing, in hough and split chest. Whatever its condition or state, being is silver-branch being. But yes, you are right, altered perception must mean and will mean altered behaviour.'

'The sea being what it is in his perception of it doesn't deter Manannán from riding over it in a four-horse chariot,' the druid said.

'So?'

'So we might as well live in the world as it used to be.'

'To talk about the world as it used to be is to talk about our eyes and minds as they used to be,' Bran said.

Manannán did come ashore.

Sometimes those who lived far away from people would see him, a silver-antlered stag walking alone.

But of all the people who lived in Ireland at that time only Bran was willing to pay the price of conversion to silver-branch seeing and knowing.

And that to this day is what Ireland is.

Less and less as time goes by do the people who live in it know that Ireland is Manannán's lost cause.

Are you content that this is so?

Looking back at it from the Moon or from Mars, are you content that our planet is Manannán's lost cause?

Here at home, standing before a bush in Cnoc an Utha, can you be content with anything less than the mirum and the morality of Manannán's

At-chíu.

II

Ireland's Bhagavad Gita as a Christian Might Be Happy to Sing It

H AVING HEARD that Bran mac Feabhail had met Man-annán mac Lir, god of the sea, out at sea, St Patrick turned in at his gate or, as it turned out, at the three sequent gates of his triple-ditched ringfort, each ditch perfectly palisaded and, as though he was expected, torches lighted at all three sets of gate posts.

And yes, Bran did look like someone who had seen God. Even as he looked at you, his eyes fully on you, he was still looking seaward.

What Manannán had said to Bran, singing it out over the manes and heads of his chariot horses at sea, that is what everyone Patrick had met walking west along the road had talked about, warrior and druid and child and crone and swineherd and cattle-reaver and seeress singing it:

> Cáini amra laisin mBran
> ina churchán tar muir nglan;
> > os mé, am charput do chéin
> > is magh sccothach ima-réidh.
>
> A n-us muir glan
> don náoi broindig a tá Bran,

> *is Mag Meall co n-iumat scoth*
> *damsa a carput dá roth.*

At-chí Bran
lín tonn tibri tar muir nglan.
> *At-chíu ca-déin i mMagh Mon*
> *sgotha cennderga gin on.*

Taithnit gabra lir a sam
sella roiscc ro sire Bran.
> *Brundit sscotha sruaim do mil*
> *a crích Manannáin mic Lir.*

Lí na fairge fora taí
geldod mora imme-roí:
> *ra sert buidhe ocus glas;*
> *is talam nád écomrass.*

Lingit ích bricc ass de brú
a muir finn forn-aiccisiu;
> *it láoig it úain co ndath,*
> *co cairde, cin imarbad …*

Manannán, a god, telling Bran, a mortal, what to you is bitter sea is to me a Plain of Delights, what to you is an endless, aimless heaving this way and that is to me a perfect world, nothing in it that isn't as perfect as an otter's face or as the fragrance of a primrose.

All of this Patrick knew, having heard it so often in so many local accents as it spread across the country, turning off chariot roads onto cow tracks, onto paths through woods and to wells and from wells to every house for miles about.

'Why?' Patrick asked a man he heard singing it at a fair. 'Why do you sing it over and over and over again?'

'Because it is what it is, that's why I sing it,' he said. 'I sing it because it is a Song of God, and while I'm singing it here at the centre, be sure that it is also being sung at the four corners of Ireland. For the first time ever all royal and tribal boundaries have gone down in Ireland. For the first time ever Ireland is one.

It is one in a sung Song of God.'

And again, crowds around him, he began:

> *Cáini amra laisin mBran*
> *ina churchán tar muir nglan;*
> > *os mé, am charput do chéin*
> > *is magh sccothach ima-réidh.*

What Patrick wasn't at all sure of, even though he had heard so much about it, was the silver branch. What had it to do with all of this? When and how did it first appear? Its music, could anyone endure it? Was it still among us? Had it come to stay? And if it had, what would that mean? A totally new way of understanding ordinary things? A totally new way, or perhaps a dangerously new way, of relating to river and star? The silver branch among us? Was that Manannán's way of seeing things among us? Is reality our way of seeing it or Manannán's way of seeing it? And if it is as Manannán sees it how can we ever pick it off a briar to feed ourselves, how can we ever chop it to warm ourselves, how when we need to piss can we so far dare as to actually piss on it? Or is it that the singing of the silver branch is in our pissing too? Is our pissing a Song of God? The Song of God the man sang at the fair?

> *A n-us muir glan*
> *don náoi broindig a tá Bran,*
> > *is Mag Meall co n-iumat scoth*
> > *damsa a carput dá roth …*

Is this the Pagan Gospel?

Patrick needed to know and that was why, night falling on him, he walked through all three torch-lit gates and, sitting in front of him, put these two questions to Bran: 'How perfect is an otter's face when he has a brown trout between his teeth? What does the trout think?'

'A strange thing happened to me one day,' Bran said. 'For the first time in my life I felt a big inconvenient need to be on my own, and silence, I wanted to know what that was like. At the cost of my people thinking that something bad was happening to me, I walked out and down and away into the wetlands, and yes, there was silence there, and solitude, more of both of them than I felt I could take. It was hard on me. Anything I could hurl a spear at or take a sword to I could deal with, but how having beaten it back, how having cornered it, could I shove a sword in solitude. For the first time in my long warrior's life I knew defeat. 'Twas as if, cupping my hand down into it, I had drunk defeat. Me? Me defeated? Me defeated, not by Ferdia, but by solitude? Me defeated, not by Cú Chulainn, but by silence? Would they see it in me? My people, would they see that I had been defeated, it making no difference by what? And what then of their continuing willingness to be led by me, to be ruled by me? Where normally I'd have turned for home I turned that day to come back and face insurgency. Then, listening downheartedly to the plashing of my feet in water as I walked, I heard it, a music surely not of our world. Even my bones, even my mind. I thought it would melt. Turning round, I saw a silver branch, and it wasn't that it was making the music as a singer or as a harper might. It was the music. In its very being it was the music. It threatened me in all that I was. Not laying a hand on me, it raided me. Listening to it, if what I was doing was listening to it, I died to all habits of eye and mind in me. Listening to it, for a moment, only for a moment, I mattered as little to me as I do every night in dreamless sleep. Not because it had mercy on me, it ceased. Eventually, enough of who and what I used to be came back to me, and I walked home.

'Caring not at all what druid or warrior or poet or harper or smith might think, I sat in silence that night, our usual bright life going on all around me.

'Suddenly, in the middle of loud but good-humoured uproar there was silence. Withdrawing my hand from before my eyes, I saw a woman surely not of our world and what startled me was that her singing was the singing of the silver branch. Having no care for us, having no mercy on us, fifty quatrains she sang celebrating the world she came from and, the thing seeming like a doom to me, she invited me, or was it that she commanded me, to come and live in it.

'Next morning, a company of three times nine warriors in each of three ships, we put out to sea, a spitting, wet wind of two minds where it wanted to blow from making life hard for us. After a day and a night our hands felt pickled. By evening it was our eyes, and soon, the way things were going, it would be our minds.

'We toiled all night and, every ship's length of headway hard to hold on to, we toiled all morning, and then, hearing the thunder of him coming, we saw him, Manannán mac Lir, god of the sea, coming over the sea.

'Out over the manes and heads of his chariot horses he sang, Manannán singing to us, or, you could say, it was the silver branch singing to us, or, yet again, you could say that it was reality itself that was singing to us, telling us that it isn't as we perceive it:

> *At-chí Bran*
> *lín tonn tibri tar muir nglan.*
> > *At-chíu ca-déin i mMagh Mon*
> > *sgotha cennderga gin on.*

'And what surprised us all the more, and frightened us all the more, was this: still singing to us out over the manes and heads of his thunder horses, Manannán, god of the sea, telling us that he will soon come ashore into Ireland, not to appear to us, but to lie with a woman called Caointigirn. As he sang of him, his singing the singing of the silver branch, we could see him, the Son of God who would be born among us, who would walk among us:

> *Moidfid sognáis gach sídhe;*
> *bid treitil cach daghthíre;*
> > *at-fii rúna rith ecne*
> > *isin mbith can a ecli.*

> *Bieid hi fethol cech míl*
> *itir glasmuir ocus tír;*

> bid druac re mbuidnib hi froiss;
> bid cú allaid cech indroiss.

Bid damh co mbennuiph argait
hi mruig i nd-agthar carpait;
> bid écni brec, i llinn lain;
> bid rón, bid eala fionnbán.

Biaid tre bitha síora
cét mbliadna hi findrighe;
> silis learca lecht imchían;
> dergfaid roí roth imrían.

'He will be welcome in all worlds and in all dimensions of any one world. To all mysteries and secrets he will have answers. When he needs to, he will be a dragon, he will be a wolf. Not limiting himself to one way, to one way only, of experiencing himself and the world, he will be a speckled salmon in a pool that mirrors mountains. The sea calling him, he will be a seal. A swan in a lake alone he will be. Seeing a silver-antlered stag walking to a river to drink, a swineherd will say to his fellow, that's him, that's the Son of God. Riding into it in a jewelled, four-horse chariot, he will redden a battlefield, fighting evil. Not just for thirty or sixty or seventy years will he live among us. No tree sown in the year of his birth will outlast him. People will think of him as they do of rivers and mountains, always with us.'

'Having heard as much as I was able to hear about reality and about our life with the Silver-Antlered Son of God, I commanded the captains to turn our ships round.

'An emanation of reality as it is, the silver branch ascended the shingles into Ireland with us.

'It was to the land we had always lived in that the woman, one of our own, had invited us.

'In every ordinary branch, whether oak branch or ash branch, is the singing of the silver branch.

'Just as well that I didn't know that day that I was setting out on the most difficult of voyages, the voyage to where we are.

'More terrible than wonderful it is that our

Song of God

is about ourselves and our world, about our eyes and everything they see, about the holes in the sides of our heads and everything they hear, about our hands and everything we in our greed grab.'

'This voyage to where we are, it's what everyone all over Ireland is talking about,' Patrick said. 'And they aren't only talking about it. Either they are turning their ships and their lives around or, the silver branch coming up the shingle shore before them, they are coming home to where they already are. It's to a state of eye and mind they are coming home. And ask anyone anywhere in Ireland now to sing a song and it's our

Song of God

they will sing.

'Ireland, for now, is a voyage, it is Bran's voyage to where we are. Indeed a man I met on the road welcomed me not to Ireland but to

BRAN'S VOYAGE TO WHERE WE ARE

'It is what they are calling Ireland now, they are calling it

Imram Brain

'You are welcome', he said, 'to silver-branch seeing and to silver-branch knowing. And you are welcome', he said, 'to settle here. To settle here', he added, 'in the delighting knowledge that the Silver-Antlered Son of God is with us, is one of us. And it isn't only us who can say that. Seals say it. Wolves say it. Swans say it. Deer say it. Dragons say it. Singing it in every branch, trees say it. The shingles of the shore you climbed coming here say it.'

'And you,' Bran asked, 'do you say it?'

'It will delight me, as it now so obviously delights everyone, when I am able to say it,' Patrick said.

'There is a question I would ask you,' Patrick said.

'Ask it,' Bran said.

'What do you do when you need to piss?'

'I go out and I piss.'

'With no sense of sacrilege against the singing of the silver branch in the grass you piss on?'

'The singing of the silver branch isn't in one thing and not in another,' Bran said. 'It is in everything, even in the cancer that is killing me.'

'Now, the full moon lighting my way, I go north,' Patrick said.

'North to where?' Bran asked.

'North to a scatter of people who live near Foclut Wood.'

'And what, might I ask, is your business with them?'

'I will talk to them about the Son of God who knows what it is to be a brown trout in an otter's mouth.'

'Then there is a further question I would ask you,' Bran said.

'Ask it,' Patrick said.

'That scatter of people who live near Foclut Wood – will you sing Manannán's song to them? Will you induct them into silver-branch seeing and knowing?'

'More likely', Patrick said, 'that they will induct me, challenging me as Christ does to consider the lily of the field, the twig on my path.'

'So why are you a Christian?'

'I have told you, haven't I?'

'Tell me again.'

'The coincidence of silver-branch ontology and savagery in an otter's teeth, in my own teeth.'

Epilogue

IT IS a strange thing. In a country to the south and east of us and a long way off if you had to walk to it, a god overshadowed a girl and a son was born to her and in time peoples and histories and languages and cultures around the world were changed by this.

Here in Ireland, to prepare us for his coming, a god sent silver-branch perception before him into our world. As a gift to us, he offered us his divine way of seeing things and knowing things. In truth, he offered us something that was native to us. Native to us, yes, but so utterly lost to us that we had by now no intimations of it asleep or awake, indoors or outdoors. The songs we sang and the stories we told had not remembrance of it. Brutally, as though it didn't exist, we felled forests, we killed and slaughtered calves, we set fire to whole mountainsides of heather and furze. We would look at a child and say 'it', what's its name. In our dealings with ourselves and our world 'it' was the predominant pronoun. Culturally conditioned to be so, our eyes were brain tumours, blue and brown, of economic seeing. Extruded or deep-set, they saw things as commodities and anything that wasn't already a commodity or couldn't be turned into a commodity, that we didn't see.

And then, insurgently, as though things would shake off our oppressive perceptions of them, the silver branch emerged among us and, soon after that, at fairs and at wells and at night along chariot roads, we were singing a new Song of God and the god whose song it was, as he announced at sea, he came ashore and now, audibly in everything everywhere, was the ontological singing of the silver branch and he fathered a Son of God, not on a goddess, not on Éire, not on Áine, not on Clíodhna, but on one of ourselves, on a woman who could be a next door neighbour to anyone, and her son, a Son of God, he was with us for up to a hundred years and he was welcome across dreadful thresholds into all worlds and when he needed to be he would be a swan or a seal or a dragon and often, reminding us that we should keep our distance, he would be a silver-antlered stag and then we would only ever see him from a long way off, walking between woods, or on a mountain ridge, in full silhouette upon the face of a full moon.

All of this happened in Ireland but for some reason news of it was not carried to the ends of the earth.

At home or abroad, no one died in its cause.

It had no Columba founding it in Scotland, no Columbanus founding it in the Alps.

It didn't bring down distant empires of thought and feeling.

Gaelic, for the reason that Manannán spoke it, didn't become a universal sacred language.

How come the silver branch isn't a sacred symbol in every land?

How come the silver branch isn't everyone's epistemology, everyone's ontology? An ontology and an epistemology that would be the double yet single source of the world's first new morality since the Pleistocene, since the catastrophe depicted in the pit in Lascaux.

If we need a vision that can open a future alternative to the one predetermined by our past, we have it, the silver branch.

The silver branch and the Holy Grail: while being singular and unique in themselves, they nonetheless have reference to everything. While being the particular thing that it is, the Grail is a way of seeing no matter what thing, a sock or a sod of turf.

Similarly, its singing the singing of everything, of sock and sod of turf, the silver branch is a universal ontology, an epiphany come among us of what everything essentially and fundamentally is, and that of course is why Bran mac Feabhail called to his captains to turn their ships round – it was to silver-branch perception as such, whether here at home or elsewhere, that the woman had invited him.

Inviting Bran, she invited all of us. But, after an initial reluctance followed by widespread excitement, we forgot about it and went back to our old ways. Eye-altering, mind-altering, world-altering event that it was, it didn't enter and shape our history in the way that tool-using did, in the way that the domestication of fire did, in the way that the move from hunting-gathering to agriculture did. Why? Could it be that silver-branch perception made excessive and in the end unbearable moral demands on us? How if you know it in its ontological excellence, can you take an axe to a tree? How, if you can hear the singing of the silver branch in it, can you eat the food in front of you, on your own table at home on a ordinary day or on the Table Rownde at Camelot on Pentecost Sunday, 'four hundred wyntir and four and fyffty aftir the Passion of Oure Lorde Jesu Chryst'? How, if it is a Syege Perelous, can you come in after a hard day's work and sit on your own chair by your own fire? Is it that, while silver-branch perception is momentarily bearable, silver-branch morality is, even momentarily, unbearable? Whatever the reason, the greatest event in our history didn't shape our history. Wiser than Bran, St Patrick knew that it is only in Paradise that a paradisal morality is possible. Here, in what can only be a fallen world, even if we perceive them paradisally we must at the same time perceive the savagery in another's teeth, and, for some, in that perception alone is Passion. Passion in the Christian sense. As well as being delighted by the world, as Jesus was, so, like Him, can we be sore amazed by it.

Bran mac Feabhail came in off the sea from the west with astounding good news. St Patrick came in off the sea from the east with astounding good news. What an astounding place Ireland would be if, in it, we learned to sing what they separately came ashore with as single Good News.

Great poet though he was, Rilke could only bring himself to say, song is existence. But, on the night that Manannán came ashore and walked across Ireland, everyone listening to everything knew that existence is song. And so, if by chance you wander over a border into a dimension of Ireland called Éire and if someone asks you where you come from, then, surely, you will play one of the great airs on your fiddle and, having played it, you will say, that's where I come from, and, although your present circumstances are a distraction, that too is where you come from, and what is more, even while he is singing his Song of Himself, it is where Bear comes from, even while he is howling, it is where Wolf comes from, even while they are fighting for the crown, it is where Wolf and Bear and Boy come from and so:

Ailiu iath n-hErend
Hermach hermach muir
Mothach mothach sliab
Srathach srathach caill
Cithach cithach aub
Essach essach loch.

Book Two

IRELAND, ULTIMATELY

Preface

YEATS puts it up to us in his 1926 essay 'The Need for Audacity of Thought':

> The intellect of Ireland is irreligious, it is not possible to select from any Irish writer of the last two hundred years until the present generation, a solitary sentence that might be included in a reputable anthology of religious thought. Ireland has not produced a religious genius since Johannes Scotus Origena, who wrote in all probability under the influence of philosophical Greek and Roman refugees of the fourth and fifth centuries, and its moral system being without intellectual roots has shown of late that it cannot resist the onset of modern life. We have had murders, authorized and 'unauthorized', burnings and robberies; we are quick to hate and slow to love; and we have never lacked a Press to excite the most evil passions. To some extent Ireland has shown in an acute form the European problem, and must seek a remedy where the best minds of Europe seek it – in audacity of speculation and creation.

Thinking of Ireland in megalithic times: Newgrange is audacity of thought and of action; aesthetically and religiously more tremendous than the Parthenon, Labby Rock in Sligo is audacity of thought and of action.

Coming forward to Celtic times: our fight with the Súil Mildagach and the Nemtenga is audacity of thought and of action; our Bhagavad Gita sung to us at sea by the god of the sea is audacity of thought and of action; dolmen love is audacity of thought and of action; Fír Flathemon is audacity of thought and of action; Énflaith is audacity of thought and of action; living from what the whole psyche knows is audacity of thought and of action; as Cú Roí mac Daire enacted it, metanoesis is audacity of thought and of action, is audacity beyond thought and beyond action.

Coming forward to modern times: a poem called 'Byzantium' is audacity of thought and of action; the conversion of a military winding stair into the mystical ascent is audacity of thought and of action.

Also, an anthology of religious thought will be all the more reputable for including this Mahadeviyaka out of Ireland:

At stroke of midnight soul cannot endure
A bodily or a mental furniture

Having enacted it, it could be Cú Roí who said it.

In Ireland from the beginning it is philomythically that we have been philosophical.

In Ireland Manannán is our Socrates, Lugh is our Descartes and Cú Roí is our Kant.

In Ireland we do not talk about the Good. Rather do we delight in thinking about Cormac, he in spite of awful instincts to the contrary becoming and, in the end, being, a good man.

In Ireland long ago, our anthropology not so anthropocentric, we lived not in a republic but in an Énflaith.

In Ireland, having walked north to Tara with Conaire, we have walked a long way past all recent revolutions.

In Ireland, every year in the golden time of the year, we ascend seeking the highest view.

In Ireland …

In Ireland …

In Ireland …

Roman geographers believed that Ireland was one of the ultimate islands of the world. To be geographically ultimate must surely challenge us to be ultimate philosophically and spiritually. Surely it must challenge us to live ultimately to ultimate purpose.

It is a journey like no other.

Let us set out only when we can do so from a place below nerve in us.

'The dangers of life are many, and safety is one of them,' said Goethe.

Yes, but audacity of nerve and therefore of the nervous kind could be a pitfall, could be an

abyss fall

on this road.

On a Mandukya morning, even between the Divine Paps of Divine Danu, it is all too trespassingly easy to set off an avalanche that neither you nor anyone else will hear.

You have taken my east from me,
And you have taken my west from me;
You have taken all that was before me from me,
And all that was behind me from me;
You have taken the moon from me,
And you have taken the sun from me,
And 'tis my great fear that you have taken my God from me.

Crunncú is portent: in our dealings with goddess or god, even when our blindness is in some ways voyant, we can get things calamitously wrong.

In the sound of hooves on his floor, in the sound of hooves in his yard, in that divine but thankless and cruel neighing back from the hills – suddenly and irretrievably in all of this there was for Crunncú a destroying enlightenment.

And Crunncú didn't have an Antigone for a daughter, and even if he had there was in his world no Colonus Wood to which she could guide him

And if we can get things this far wrong with Macha, think how wrong we can get things with Cú Roí, think how wrong we can get things crossing the Torrent with Jesus.

Walk on, but be prepared: this time round it could be in ghoramurti mood that Lugh and Manannán and Danu will show themselves to us.

For all his sincere, half-savage devotion, Crunncú was hippoluted in a way that Hippolytus wasn't.

If you have heeded the warning, walk on in your anodos into

ULTIMATE IRELAND

a land the Celts, following Amhairghin Glúngheal, have yet to cross into.

Lugh

IRELAND was in a sorry state at the time. A terrible, spectral people called the Fomorians had come ashore and there was now no river or valley or mountain or plain that wasn't the worse for their coming. They were spectral not because they didn't originally have bodies. Spirit gone bad in them had sucked and aggrandized their bodies into its hectic hunger for supremacy over all things. Wraiths of themselves though they were, they smouldered and burned, even for things they didn't need, for things which, in the acquisition, could only impede them. Also, what people made moderate by their bodies wouldn't do, they would do. Within a few years of their coming, the land itself was a wraith of itself, spectral and ghostly, in most places ghastly, and in all of this their leader and exemplar was Balar, he of the evil eye. In one of Ireland's oldest books this eye is called the

Súil Mildagach

Single in Balar, it is the collective Fomorian eye and so deadly with death-rays is it to anything it looks upon it has to be covered, asleep and awake, not just by its own lid but by a constructed lid of nine occluding layers, each a layer that would wholly eclipse the noonday sun.

In all that they were and in all that they did, the Fomorians were as different as could be from the Tuatha Dé Danann, a people a long time resident in the land. Only no. Not just resident. So at one with the land were they, you could walk through it and not know they were in it. Now they were in trouble. In trouble if they didn't fight. In trouble if they fought.

They only had to think of Balar's eye, at first emerging, and then, fully emerged, from its eclipse.

What, with their wizardries, could wizards do to reverse those death-rays, red and black? What, with their weapons, could warriors do?

Since it would be irreverent to do so, no one asked why, or why now, but it would ever afterwards be remembered as the greatest thing that had so far happened in Ireland. More. As well as being the greatest thing that had so far happened in Ireland it would be remembered as the greatest thing that had so far happened to it.

It would be called

The Coming of Lugh

The coming of a god called Lugh.

Other gods came and went. Not Lugh.

Not jealous of his transcendence, Lugh condescended to immanence in religion, in ritual.

It was like a man looking for work or, some would say, it was as a man looking for work, that he came among mortals.

Falling in with people along the way, asking people the way, he came to the king's door in Tara.

Gamal mac Figail, the doorkeeper, challenged him: 'What art do you practice? For no one without an art enters Tara.'

'Question me,' Lugh said, 'I am a builder.'

'We have a warrior,' the doorkeeper answered, 'we do not need you, we have a builder already, Luchta mac Luachada.'

Lugh said, 'Question me, doorkeeper: I am a smith.'

The doorkeeper answered him, 'We have a smith already, Colum Cúaléinech of the three techniques.'

'Question me,' Lugh said, 'I am a champion.'

The doorkeeper answered, 'We do not need you. We have a champion already, Ogma mac Ethlend.'

'Question me,' Lugh said, 'I am a harper.'

'We do not need you,' Gamal said, 'we have a harper already, Abcán mac Bicelmois, whom the men of the three gods chose in the sid-mounds.'

'Question me,' Lugh said, 'I am a warrior.'

'We do not need you,' Gamal mac Figail, the doorkeeper, said, 'we already have a warrior, Bresal Eterlam mac Echdach Baethlaim.'

'Question me,' Lugh said, 'I am a poet and a historian.'

'We do not need you,' the doorkeeper said. 'We already have a poet and historian, Én mac Ethamain.'

'Question me,' Lugh said, 'I am a sorcerer.'

'We do not need you,' the doorkeeper said, 'we have sorcerers already. Our druids and our people of power are numerous.'

A god seeking entrance into human affairs, Lugh continued.

'Question me,' he said, 'I am a physician.'

'We do not need you,' Gamal said, 'we have Dien Cecht, the best of physicians.'

'Question me,' Lugh said, 'I am a cupbearer.'

'We do not need you,' the doorkeeper said, 'we have cupbearers already: Delt and Drúcht and Daithe, Tae and Talom and Trog, Glé and Glan and Glésse.'

'Question me,' the god said, 'I am a brazier.'

'We do not need you,' the doorkeeper said, 'we have a brazier already, Crédne Cerd.'

'Ask the king,' the god said, 'if he has one man who is master in all these arts: if he has I will not be able to enter Tara.'

Going into the royal hall, Gamal told the king that a samildanach, a man skilled in all arts, was at the door.

'Try him at fidchel,' Nuadu, the king, said.

Lugh won against the best who came out to challenge him.

'Let him in,' the king said, 'for a man like him has never before come into our hall, in this, our triple-ditched ringfort.'

Then the doorkeeper did as he had been bidden, and Lugh came in and sat in the suide súad, the chair or seige of the sage, for, as the old book has it, 'bo suí cacha dáno é', this meaning that he was not only skilled but sage in all arts.

Now that they had on their side someone who could take on Balar in battle, the Tuatha Dé Danann decided that they would seek to drive the Fomorians from the land.

It would be a battle between a people intent on shaping nature to suit them and a people who, surrendering to it, would let nature shape them to suit it.

First it was a battle of wizards launching killing curses across a no-man's-land at each other.

Then it was sorcerers wolf-howling, bull-bellowing and otter-snarling delusions at each other.

Then it was witches conjuring wild winds to blow the steam from their cauldrons upon each other.

Then it was poets seeking to shame each other to despair and death.

Then:

Harsh was the noise made by the multitude of warriors and champions protecting their swords and shields and bodies while others were striking them with spears and swords. Harsh too the tumult all over the battlefield – the shouting of the warriors and the clashing of bright shields, the swish of swords and ivory-hilted blades, the clatter and rattling of the quivers, the hum and whirr of spears and javelins, the crashing strokes of weapons. As they hacked at each other their fingertips and their feet almost met; and because of the slipperiness of the blood under the warrior's feet, they kept falling down and their heads were cut off as they sat there. A gory, wound-inflicting, sharp, bloody battle was upheaved, and spearshafts were reddened in the hands of foes.

Then comes a moment that can never be forgotten, even in Ireland. It is best if we hear it first in the old words of the old book:

Imma-comairnic de Luc ocus di Bolur Birugderc esin cath.

In English it reads:

Lugh and Balar of the piercing eye met in the battle.

Its lid had just been lifted off Balar's eye, but Lugh wasn't found wanting. The stone he released from his sling smashed into it, driving it all the way back through the hideously huge head so that it was now sending its death-rays, red and black, against his own people, withering them, shrivelling them, killing them in their thousands.

The battle between two peoples had now come down to this: to single combat between Balar and Lugh.

They fought each other for days, and for weeks, all over Ireland, north as far as the sea, south to the centre, east to the sea, west to the sea, back to the centre, south to the sea, and there it was, on Carn Uí Néit overlooking the sea, that Lugh twisted Balar's battered head off his battered body. The head spoke, telling Lugh that if he would set it upon his own head all of its power would flow down into him. Alert to the deception, Lugh set it upon a rock. A last drop of poison draining down on to it, the rock shattered. Looking back from a high horizon, Lugh saw three of them seven of them, ten of them, ten carrion crows he saw, circling.

Lugh went on to become king of Ireland.

Ireland, in his day, was a Kingdom of God.

Curiously, though, it was only when he retired from the sensory scene that we began to recognize him and honour him for the very great god that he was.

Calling it Lughnasadh in his honour, we assigned to him a full lunar month of our liturgical year. Harvest time, it was the golden time.

At the beginning of this, the golden time, we would ascend to the summit of the local high place.

It mattered not at all whether our local high place was a hill or a mountain. Spiritually, since it was Lugh we would honour up there, the summit of a hill was of a height with the summit of a mountain.

Lugh was the god of the higher view.

He was god of the golden time and the higher view.

And all year long, at home in the lowlands, we would live in the golden time and from the higher view.

The golden time and the higher view, they were our mantras.

Morning, noon and night we would chant them:

> I live in the golden time
> The golden time I am
>
> I live from the higher view
> The higher view I am.

And if someone fell sick we would ascend our hill for them.

Setting foot on it, we would say, 'In the name of God and for the sake of everyone who needs the higher view.'

It is how we understood sickness. We understood it as the fading out of the higher view.

For some it was Lughnasadh all year round.

All year round they lived in the golden time.

Then, as with all things earthly, a decline.

In the sense that it is the collective eye concentrated in one eye, the Súil Mildagach grew back and flourished again.

This time, Lugh didn't come to Tara seeking redemptive re-entry into human affairs.

All too soon, we who had driven out the Fomorians were ourselves Fomorians.

Only Ogma, something not known sustaining him, didn't capitulate.

Macha

HAD HE, under tutelage, disciplined the savagery that was in him, and the generosity that was in him, Crunncú might have been a great warrior. As it turned out, he ended up alone, discovering once to his cost that he hadn't, like his cattle, lost his wildness.

Afterwards, as much as he could, he avoided fairs. And assemblies of his people at Bealtaine and Samhain, and assemblies in honour of Crom Dubh, them also he stayed away from.

His four unbroken horses coming down the hillside after her, she came. His door was open.

'I'll be a woman to you,' she said, going to the fire and putting fresh logs on it.

Wild though she was, one of the horses put her head through the door.

Not wishing to give the impression that his house was a stable, or that he lived with his animals, Crunncú went towards her, threatening her.

She didn't move.

The horse and the woman looked at each other.

They looked a long time at each other.

At exactly the same moment, nothing overtly happening between them, the woman turned to her work, the horse backed away, and realizing he was out of his depth, Crunncú asked no questions.

Unsure of himself, he went out.

He stayed out all day, gathering his dry cattle and herding them to higher grazing ground.

The higher view didn't help him.

Heights today didn't mean elevation of thought or of feeling. Being higher than the highest wild goat, being higher than a peregrine falcon bringing wool to her nest, to Crunncú up there looking down on his life's work that meant, not delight, but defeat. Bracken and furze had all but taken over his world. Yet, even now, when last year's bracken was tinder dry, he wouldn't fire it. The fired bracken would fire the furze, but the thought of all that wildness going up in smoke, that was a price he wouldn't pay. Wild nature outside him, letting it be, that was his sacrifice of appeasement to wild nature inside him. Religiously, in ways such as this, Crunncú coped.

Shoulder deep in furze, flowering now, he walked back to his house.

A changed house it was.

Nothing had been altered, nothing disturbed, not even the five cobwebs in the five hanging bridles had been molested. And that reassured him. In firelight, now as always, they looked like death masks. Masks of something dead in himself, he sometimes thought.

No, in outward appearance nothing had changed. And yet, particularly at threshold and hearth, it was as if the house had undergone rededication. But to what he didn't know.

Who is she, he wondered, watching her skimming the evening's milk.

Had she come bringing last year's last sheaf of corn, he'd have though she was the Corn Caillech.

Had she come, walking tall and naked, and holding a spear, he'd have thought she was Scathách.

Had she come, a lone skald crow calling above her, he'd have thought she was the Badhbh Catha.

Had she, having come, opened her thighs and showed her vast vulva he'd have thought she was Sheela-na-gig.

Awake, he wondered.

Asleep, he wondered.

Who is she, he wondered, watching her rear like a horse in his dreams.

And the horse that so regularly came to stand in his door? Shoulder deep in the morning, hip deep in the evening, what did that portend?

There was, he sensed, something he knew about her. But he knew it only where it was safe to know it, in dreamless sleep.

And he wasn't a man to her yet. And in the way that a woman is sometimes a woman to a man, she had so far showed no sign that she wanted to be a woman to him in that welcome way.

And how could any man be a man to a woman like her? How, he looking at her, and she looking at him, could he lay a desiring hand upon her? Would she, showing her teeth, rear like a horse as she did in his dreams?

Sitting across from her by the fire one evening, something dawned on him: until she came his house had sheltered him, but only as a shed might shelter a cow. Like a religion now, it sheltered him inwardly. Like a religion that was there from the beginning, like a religion that had grown with the growing world, it sheltered him in his difficult depths.

It was strange.

> A horse, and she not broken, standing shoulder deep
> in his door every morning
> A horse, and she not broken, standing hip deep
> in his door every evening.

From hip deep in his nature the dream came: walking high moors he was when he came upon it, the tall standing stone. Taller than a man, it was a man's member, or a god's member, and it was suffering. As a woman in labour suffers, it was suffering. And then, up from the roots a shuddering came, upwards it shuddered, upwards it surged into a long releasing scream that awakened Crunncú, and lying there he knew that in some strange way he had been a man to the woman who was lying beside him.

'Welcome to the great world,' she said.

Terror of what had happened was shaking Crunncú.

Till dawn it continued, shaking the shaken foundations of old established mind in him, of old established mood in him.

'I'm ruined,' he said.

'Walk through the ruins,' she said.

'Walk through the ruins you've already walked through.

'Walk in the great world you've already walked into.'

'It's a nothing, a nowhere, I've walked into,' he said.

'No more marvellous place than that nothing, that no-where,' she said. 'It's God,' she said. 'It's the Divine behind God, behind all gods,' she said. 'It's the Divine out of which the gods and the stars are born,' she said.

'My name is Macha,' she said.

For the first time since waking Crunncú opened his eyes, opened them in anger, in dangerous, frightened anger.

'We should never call anyone Macha but Macha,' he blazed.

'Do you hear me? We should never call anyone Macha but Macha. Macha's name is a holy name. It belongs to no one but Macha. To no one, no one. To no one but Macha.'

His anger became religious indignation, he fixed her in a cold stare: 'Your name isn't Macha! In this house it isn't Macha. I keep horses for Macha. In honour of Macha, in praise of Macha, in thanksgiving to Macha, I never, not even in a moment of greed, attempt to bridle them, I never attempt to break them in. Wild on the hills, neighing on the hills, their manes and their tails streaming in the hills, they are the glory of Macha. They are the nearest we can ever come, safely come, to a vision of Macha.

In her nature Macha
In her name Macha

'Sharing neither nature nor name with anyone, that is Macha. Taking Macha's name you have sinned against Macha. Taking Macha's name you aren't safe to sit with, you aren't safe to eat with, you aren't safe to lie with. What I cannot understand is why our cow hasn't run dry, why our well hasn't run dry. In my house, no! In my house your name is not Macha.'

'By what name then shall I be known?'

'By the name of my neighbour's nag.'

'What's her name?'

'She has no name. Nag is her name. And it's your name. Until you find favour with Macha, it is your name. Nag is your name! Nag!'

'And how might that be? How might I find favour with Macha?'

'That's for Macha to decide. She might never decide. Macha's heart can be hoof hard. And her head! No! Macha's holy head has never been bridled. Cobwebs blind the bridles we would bridle Macha with. The bridles we would bridle Macha with are masks of our own terror. Attempt to bridle Macha as you'd attempt to bridle an ordinary horse, attempt it, just that, and your face will fall in, into nothingness, into emptiness, into your own empty skull looking back at you as a bridle hanging on a stable wall would.

Macha is lovely
Macha is ugly

Macha is gentle
Macha is vicious

Macha has arms
Macha has hooves

'The most beautiful of women is Macha: she opens her thighs and you see a mare's mouth.

Macha is Life
Macha is Death

Bigger than the life we live is Macha
Bigger than the death we die is Macha
With no ritual have we bridled Macha.

With no religion have we broken her in.
In no temple to Macha have we stabled Macha.
Everything in the world that we aren't able for, that's Macha.
Everything in ourselves that we aren't able for, that's Macha.
Everything religion isn't able for, everything culture isn't able for,
that's Macha.

Stories we have that can cope with Crom Dubh.
No story we have or ever will have can cope with Macha.

'Search our stories, our Táins and Toraiochts, and in them
you'll find not a hoof-mark of Macha, in them you'll not find a
shake of her tail.

'No! No! Neither Táin nor Toraiocht has covered Macha.
Rising on its hind legs like a stallion, our Aill at Uisnech hasn't
covered Macha.

'Living in a world as wild as this one is, the only goddess or
god I leave a door open for, and leave a fire on for, is a goddess
or god who hasn't submitted to our sanctimonies and sacra-
ments, who hasn't submitted to religion. And that's Macha.

For Macha I leave my door open.
For Macha I leave my fire lighting at night.

Macha hasn't been covered by culture.
Macha hasn't been covered by religion.

'Who or what could cover Macha?' he asked.
'You have covered Macha,' she replied.
Outraged and afraid, he was on the floor pulling on his
clothes and his boots.
Hearing her walk away, he looked up.
Hearing hooves on the yard, he went to the door.
It was May Morning and Crunncú knew, too late he knew,
that it wasn't his neighbour's nag who neighed from the hills.

Manannán and Crom Dubh

A DREAM: after awful, near-universal slaughter in Magh Tuired, it came down to a fight to the death between Balar and Lugh. Fearing the worst, I closed my eyes. Then, accepting the worst, I opened them, and instantly I was charmed. Instead of carnage from horizon to horizon and red-mouthed carrion crows everywhere eating the unseeing eyes of wizards and warriors, this was Magh Meall, this was the Plain of Delights, and at the heart of it Manannán was singing to Balar. By the end of his song all the dead had come back to life and in everyone, even in Balar, Súil Mildagach seeing had become silver-branch perception, not just in the sense of sight but in all our senses.

More glorious than when it was a Kingdom of God, than when it was the Kingdom of Lugh, Ireland tonight was the real Isle of Man, the real

Isle of Manannán

the isle in which he fathered a Son of God on Caointigirn, our neighbour.

And did those feet ...?

They did, and we aren't only talking about Manannán's feet.

Lugh walked here.

Macha walked here.

Cú Roí walked here.

Danu walked here.

Stooped but bringing the first sheaf of corn on his back into Ireland, Crom Dubh walked here.

Sometimes someone who lived alone in an out-of-the-way place would hear footsteps in his yard. He'd look up and that would be him, the stooped One, walking past his window.

St Patrick and Crom Dubh fell into religious contention.

Crom Dubh had a mighty black bull. St Patrick only had his copy of the scriptures.

They agreed that they would weigh the bull against a single verse of scripture.

The verse proved heavier, but that did not mean the end either of Crom Dubh or of his bull or of paganism in Ireland. To this day Crom Dubh has a Sunday in his honour. It is called Domhnach Crom Dubh, Crom Dubh's Sunday, and it is only recently that an old stone head of him was stolen from a Christian church, now a graveyard ruin, in Clochán under Mount Brandon on Dingle peninsula. There are local people who would very much like to have him back. And, thinking no doubt of his own little cobwebbed patch of light, an old man has complained that windows out west aren't at all what they used to be.

In his 'Hymn on the Morning of Christ's Nativity' Milton sent all pagan gods, all fays, all spirits of river and wood down into hell.

What Milton puritanically did in religion Descartes puritanically did in philosophy.

We are talking about a Miltonic-Cartesian clean sweep.

It hasn't been good for rivers and for woods.

It hasn't been good for us.

In that it allows for pious rememberance, Domhnach Crom Dubh is a wiser response to what, admittedly, is an event so stupendous that all traditions of thought, including the biblical, are at a loss what to say or do.

Even so, cobwebbed though it is, the old pagan window can still fenestrate our lives with sacred sea-light, with sacred land-light, with the light, orient and immortal, of that first sheaf of wheat, progenitor of wind-blown gold, of gold standing still, all over the land.

What a blessing that in Ireland on one day of the year Crom Dubh's bull and a verse of Christ's gospel are of equal weight, actually, religiously and philosophically.

Manannán sings to us and here, in delighted response, gita answering gita, we sing to him.

Out of our awareness of the coincidence in us of savagery and silver-branch ontology we sing to him:

Am gaeth i mmuir
Am tond trethan
Am fuaim mara
Am dam secht ndrenn
Am séig i n-aill
Am dér gréne
Am cáin
Am torc ar gail
Am hé i llind …

We mean our song as Sir Thomas Browne would:

There is all Africa and her prodigies in us.

As Nietzsche would:

I have discovered for myself that the old human and animal life, indeed the entire prehistory and past of all sentient being works, on loves on, hates on, thinks on in me.

As Conrad would:

The mind of man is capable of anything – because every-thing is in it, all the past as well as all the future.

It's the song that Caointigirn, his bhakta, his Radha, might sing as she walks into Manannán's arms.

Even if the boar they in themselves are turns on them there, what better love-bed than Labby Rock can we imagine for them.

Not without significance is the fact that Labby Rock is the megalithic tomb of a king killed in the Battle of Magh Tuired.

In a dream of it Magh Tuired became Magh Meall, the Plain of Delights.

Among those delights are the delights of dolmen love.

We are talking about a nativity, about the birth, of a new religious sensibility in Ireland.

It is for us to compose and sing the love songs that Caointigirn and Manannán might sing to each other.

Think of Hindu India. Think of Mahadeviyaka singing to Shiva, the Lord:

If sparks fly
I shall think my thirst and hunger quelled.

If the skies tear down
I shall think them pouring for my bath.

If a hillside slide on me
I shall think it a flower for my hair.

O Lord white as jasmine, if my head falls from my
    shoulders
I shall think it your offering.

*

O mother I burned
in a flameless fire

O mother I suffered
a bloodless wound

Mother I tossed
Without a pleasure

Loving my Lord white as jasmine
I wandered through unlikely worlds

*

Husband inside,
    lover outside,
      I can't manage them both.

This world
    and that other,
      cannot manage them both.

O Lord white as jasmine

I cannot hold in one hand
    both the round nut
    and the long bow.

*

Who cares
    who strips a tree of leaf
    once the fruit is plucked?

Who cares
    who lies with the woman
    you have left?

Who cares
    who ploughs the land
    you have abandoned?

After this body has known my Lord
    who cares if it feeds
    a dog
    or soaks up water?

*

It was like a stream
    running into the dry bed
    of a lake,

like rain
pouring on plants
parched to sticks.

It was like this world's pleasure
and the way to the other,
                    both
walking towards me.

Seeing the feet of the master
O Lord white as jasmine
    I was made
    worthwhile.

Mahadeviyaka and Shiva.
Radha and Krishna.
Caointigirn and Manannán.

I think of an Ireland that comes in dreams of itself to Labby Rock and to Dá Chích Danann, an Ireland that prospers in bhakta yoga and in jnana yoga, an Ireland that prospers in bhakta-passionate love songs and in Upanishads.

Not that we can happily settle for being a Hindu India in the Atlantic.

In India as well as in Ireland, in Taoist China as well as in Aboriginal Australia, in Islam as well as in Aztec Mexico, Jesus is the difference, big as

Gaiakhty

big as

Buddh Gaia

We can settle for nothing less than the light of Buddh Gaia in that cobwebbed window in the Dingle Peninsula.

Cú Roí mac Daire

YOU LOOK UP at where he lives, in a stone fortress on the prow of a mountain, not moving of course, yet seeming to sail serenely westwards, and you think, at last a god not prone to condescension, a god who never has and never will be tempted to love human beings. Never will he be compromised in his high, indifferent divinity either by passion or compassion for human beings. Never, ever, in mounting sexual desire for her, will he turn himself into a swan and fall upon a girl gone out alone at evening to drive in the cows. Unlike Poseidon and Odysseus, never will he dignify us by a descent into enmity with us. Such is his transcendence, he never notices that worlds come and go. That a god, in his passion for us, has been willing to hang for us – no, such trivia do not come to his attention. Astronomically immense though it is to us, our universe will have come and gone, but will he have noticed? No. Indeed, that is the name by which we should know him. In an act of ultimate, un-self-interested reverence that would be good for us, we should call him

NO

Shockingly, in consequence of a shameless impulse to familiarity with their gods in Celtic myth, he has a name that you yourself or your neighbour might have, and when, after three or four days, a sea mist clears, revealing it, his house could be a chieftain's house, cloud high, but reachable from the east, along a gently rising ridge.

Not only does myth give him a name, calling him Cú Roí mac Daire, it gives him an appearance, that of a bachlach, a gigantic churl, whose mantle is a cracked and ragged ox-hide with the hair turned in, and also, with no less presumption, it tells stories about him. In myth, NO has a name and an identity. But, for all that, how perilous it would be not to continue to know him, in unknowing, as

NO

NO not in his nature. NO not in his being. Not NO to anything. NO in the Hindu sense of neti neti, meaning that since he is neither this nor that there is nothing therefore that we can say about him. In reverence neither towards him nor for him, we must fast from all talk about him. Not myth of course. Myth will not fast. At no matter what cost in truth or untruth, myth must talk. Unable to talk about NO as NO, it will talk about him or about it as Cú Roí. And maybe in this one instance, talk about Cú Roí is indeed talk about NO.

Time was, in Ulster, when three great heroes claimed the hero's portion, that being the place of honour and the choicest portion of meat at no matter whose table. So intense was the struggle between Conal Cearnach, Laeghaire Buadhach and Cú Chulainn, it looked as if soon every house would be in cinders, every field and river reddened. And no one, neither druí nor bean feasa, could decide between them. Not to speak about their wives, mighty women in their own right, none of them content to sit back and await the outcome.

It was the day of deadly stand-still before war. At noon on the day before the shortest day of the year, a gigantic churl walked through the dangerous, high, hare-lipped gates at Emuin Macha. In one hand he had a huge beheading block and in the other a huge axe, its iron head an unwashed crescent, and yet so sharp it could cut a rib of hair blowing in the wind. Having laid the block, gnarled and of yew and smooth from use, on the floor, he got down and stretched his inviting, naked neck out out out and again out upon it. Holding up the axe, flakes of gore falling from it, he called out, 'On the understanding that whoever beheads me will come back here tomorrow, at exactly this hour, so that I can return the favour.' Eager, over eager perhaps, to prove his worth, Conal Cearnach walked forward, took the axe and, wielding it rafter high, brought it whistling down, leaving Cú Roí as tall only as his own shoulders. With that Cú Roí got up, picked up his axe, his beheading block and his head and walked headlessly and unerringly south to his cloud-high house, if house you could call it, in Kerry.

On the morrow, at noon, he set down the beheading block on the floor in Emuin Macha and, in a voice that had huge, unnatural uproar in it, he called for Conal Cearnach. Not the man he was yesterday, Conal was nowhere to be seen.

Back, flat on the floor, his neck stretched out on the block, Cú Roí raised the axe saying, 'On the understanding that whoever beheads me will come back here tomorrow so that I can return the favour.' Believing in himself, Laeghaire Buadhach walked forward, took hold of the axe and, wielding it rafter high, brought it whistling down, half burying it in the block beneath the gaping neck. With that Cú Roí got up, picked up his axe, his beheading block and his head and walked headlessly and unerringly south to his cloud-high house, if house you could call it, in Kerry.

On the morrow, at noon, he set up his beheading block on the rush-covered floor in Emuin Macha and again, in a voice not all of it of our world, he called for Laeghaire Buadhach. Having discovered in the meantime that his life was a matter of considerable selfish importance to him, Laeghaire was nowhere to be seen.

Back, flat on the floor, his neck stretched out on the block, Cú Roí raised the axe and called out, 'On the understanding that whoever beheads me will be here tomorrow, at exactly this hour, so that I can return the favour.'

With perfect grace, Cú Chulainn walked forward, took hold of the axe and, wielding it rafter high, he brought it whistling down, so cleanly into the block, the head, though severed, didn't roll. With that Cú Roí got up, picked up his axe, his beheading block and his head and walked headlessly and unerringly south to his cloud-high house, if house you could call it, in Kerry.

On the morrow, at noon, he set up his beheading block on the floor in Emuin Macha and in a voice deadly in intent, he called for Cú Chulainn.

Cú Chulainn walked forward and, like a man going to bed, he lay down, stretching his neck on the block.

'Further,' Cú Roí roared. 'Stretch that neck out further.'

'Further,' he roared. 'Further, further.'

'Still further,' he roared.

In the end, so stretched out was he, a wood pigeon could fly in and out through Cú Chulainn's ribs.

And now, watching to make sure that Cú Chulainn didn't blink, he wielded the axe rafter high and he brought it whistling down, only at the last moment pulling it wide into the earth.

Cú Chulainn came to his feet and Cú Roí declared him the hero, having the right, at no matter whose table, to the hero's portion.

And that politically is what this story is about. It tells us how one of three contenders became the undisputed hero and what would otherwise have been the most destructive of all wars was avoided.

Looked at philosophically, however, the story is about a god, best named NO, walking metanoetically south through Ireland.

And so it isn't only geographically that Ireland is one of the ultimate islands of the world. The news we have for old Greek and Roman geographers is that Ireland is ultimate philosophically and spiritually.

The final philosophical eureka has been enacted here.

Here, in a spiritual sense, the hero's portion is mergence in metanoesis and in self-abeyance with the Divine.

Blessing ourselves in the stream that runs down from the cloud-high height where NO illusorily lives, let us inaugurate a new age of heroism here.

And something else:

In euhemerist days, when the old Irish gods were thought of as heroes, it was imagined that Cú Roí and Cú Chulainn fell into contention. The story has it that Cú Chulainn took to coming south in the night to pay court to Bláithíne, Cú Roí's wife. Bláithíne was charmed. Soon her fervour for the young man was equalled by her coldness towards the old man. And so, when Cú Roí was away in some far part of the world, she would pour milk into the stream near her cloud-high house and when Cú Chulainn, waiting far below in a wood, would see the whitened water he would climb to a night of love. One night, wanting once and for all to be rid of the old man, Bláithíne let Cú Chulainn in on a secret: 'Cú Roí', she told him, 'has an external soul. It resides in a salmon who lives in a well in the wood you wait in. Kill that salmon and Cú Roí will lose his strength and his vigour.' Cú Chulainn killed the salmon. Cú Roí lost his strength and his vigour. Cú Chulainn climbed to murder, and love.

The moral of the story is that our soul isn't only in ourselves. It is in the tree we are felling and in the seal pup we are clubbing to bloody death. It follows that our world doesn't only environ us. It is in us and we are in it. From this it further follows that all damage to the world is damage to ourselves and that all damage to ourselves is damage to the world.

Let us not be content with a republic. Let us reinstitute the Énflaith. Even if the bird of the Birdreign is a hawk, as it was on Scelec, let us reinstitute it.

Clearly it isn't only Amhairghin Glúngheal and Fintan mac Bochra and Ollamh Fódhla who can say

Am hé i llind
I am a salmon in a pool

Throughout all his immortal-mortal life Cú Roí could have said it.

Cú Roí's mortality was an enrichment of his immortality.

True of Cú Roí. True of all of us.

And it wasn't only Cú Roí who suffered a serglige, a loss of strength and vigour. A few years later down his dergruathar road, so did Cú Chulainn.

The trouble with Cú Chulainn was that, in spite of his totemic name, he never once condescended to draw strength from nature.

Anyway, a truth as deep as the well in which all the rivers of Ireland have their source has walked up a mountain road towards us in Kerry: Cú Roí's secret is everyone's secret.

Thanks to Bláithíne, the secret is out.

Of course the fight between Cú Chulainn and Cú Roí for the favour of a woman isn't only a fight between a young man and an old man. Phylogenetically, it is a fight between cú and cú, between wolf and wolf. More particularly, it is a fight between wolfhound and wolf, between a wolf that has capitulated to domestication and a wolf that hasn't.

In this story, for those who can hear it etymologically, there is terrible Céol Cúaine, terrible human Céol Cúaine, and still in our day it echoes off the mountains of peninsular Kerry. We must not assume that the domesticated wolf, having won the first battle, has won the war. Cú Roí has survived gotterdammerungs and when he has a mind to, wild wolf against tame wolf, he will take care of the upstart from Ulster.

But is Cú Roí sometimes at war with himself? Is the wolf that he is at war with the salmon that he is, and are both salmon and wolf at war with the human being he sometimes is?

Out of conflict of Wolf and Bear and Boy in him, Cormac mac Airt emerged into unity of being, into splendid sovereignty of being. Tragically for him and for Gráinne, Diarmaid Ó Duibhne emerged neither into unity nor sovereignty of being. The unintegrated boar in him turned on him, as he did on Adonis, sexually sheathing his tusk, so Shakespeare tells us, in his soft groin.

How afraid for Gráinne Diarmaid was whenever he took her into the unsafe love-lair of his arms!

Did Cú Roí know something of this with Bláithíne? Did Bláithíne know?

Was Cú Chulainn too extrovert to know?

Gráinne did know, but, mortally tusked by grief in the end, she'd have eloped with Diarmaid all over again. Again and again.

Is what happened on Ben Bulben the truth about what might have happened on Slieve Mish?

Looking up at her cloud-high house I say to Bláithíne, thanks to you we know Cú Roí's secret but you yourself, what, if any, is your secret? Either with the young man or the old man, did you know passion as Gráinne did?

Climbing mountains with you, Cú Roí mac Daire, crossing rivers with you, eating wild roots with you, lying down to-night on this dolmen with you, no other woman in Ireland is so much a woman as I am. Look up at them. The shining stars approve of me. They approve of us. I know it. I know it. With you I have never been in danger so great and yet I have never been so safe. Safe at the beginning of passion, in the middle of passion, and at the screaming, collapsing end of passion.

Having come this far with Cú Roí, even if he was some nights salmon-cold to your courtship, you must surely have rebuked the sapling, showing him the road north and telling him that if he must find glory to find it in battle.

Listening to the story as Fintan mac Bochra of the shapeshifts might listen to it, we wonder was the salmon a secret in more ways than one.

Among the great nights of our lives surely is the night we discover that we aren't fish-cold at the core of our soul.

Cú Roí, the god who survives gotterdammerungs, guided us to metanoesis, and that was a very great thing indeed.

Betrothed though she was to an old man and his hounds, Gráinne broke free and guided us to a new kind of love and that too was a very great thing.

On their way west, the pursuit hound-loud behind them, Diarmaid and Gráinne crossed a stream. The water splashed up and touched Gráinne's thigh and, with that, turning to her still reluctant man, she said:

'A Dhiarmaid', ar sí, 'giodh mór do chródhacht ocus do chal-macht a ccomhlannaibh ocus a ccath-láithribh, dar liom féin as dana an braon beag baoth-uisge úd ioná tú.'

'Diarmaid', said she, 'though your valour and your bravery be great in fights and in battle-stations, I think myself that the little drop of unconventional water is more daring than you are.'

Let us look at the wonder:

An braon beag baoth-uisge
The little drop of unconventional water

In that it has touched Gráinne's thigh it has touched every-one's thigh. It has touched Cú Roí's thigh and Bláithíne's thigh and Cú Chulainn's thigh, and Amhairghin's thigh, and Manan-nán's thigh and Caointigirn's thigh, and Deirdre's thigh and Naoise's thigh and Maud Gonne's thigh and Yeats' thigh. It has touched the thigh of everyone who fought at the Battle of Magh Tuired, at the Battle of the Boyne and in Dublin 1916.

Wonderful to say, it has touched Eriu's thigh.

Seeking to know what it is, we have been talking about the Irish mind.

Whatever else it is, it will not be force-married to current convention. It is passionate.

Gráinne it is who brings the Irish mind to

An Braon Beag Baoth-Uisge

Athens has Socrates, Plato and Artistotle. France has Abel-ard, Descartes and Sartre. Germany has Kant, Schopenhauer and Nietzsche. England has Bacon, Locke and Hobbes. Ireland has Manannán, Cú Roí and Gráinne.

Always in Ireland we need to sail back out over nine waves, there to listen to Manannán.

Always in Ireland we need to walk south by west with Cú Roí.

Always in Ireland, when our soul becomes what it has yet again become in our day, we need to elope with Gráinne.

We need in our day to pioneer a new route into Ireland. A route that each one of us, setting out on our own, can attempt. We ascend between the two unequal heights of Scelec Mór, we continue through Puck Fair, we continue upwards between the Paps of Danu, we walk through the bonefire of all our fighting 'I ams' and, a new central self emerging in us, we walk onwards naked to Tara, Fál, the stone phallus, screeching its recognition of our achieved royalty.

Heard in other than the traditional way, Amhairghin's Song of Himself could be taken to mean that he has fallen asunder into his phylogenetic constituents, each of them setting itself up as an independent 'I am', the spear that he is passing through the hawk that he is, the bull that he is at war with the boar that he is. In which case his journey inland must among other things be a journey into unity of being.

Especially so if it remains available to the highest transition of all, unity of being is greatly preferable to the baleful chaos of being simultaneously this, that and the other thing.

True of Cú Roí lying down to a night of love with Bláithíne. True for Cú Chulainn lying down to a night of love with Emer. True for Diarmaid lying down that last night on Labby Rock with Gráinne:

> And Diarmaid heard the howl of a hound in his sleep in the night, and he started out of his sleep and Gráinne caught hold of him and asked him what he had heard.
>
> 'The howl of a hound I heard', he replied, 'and I wonder at hearing it in the night.'
>
> 'May safe-keeping be on you,' Gráinne said. 'Lie back down into sleep and do not heed it.'
>
> Diarmaid did as she advised but he had not yet fallen asleep when he heard the howl of the hound again, and he rose up and Gráinne caught hold of him and told him not to go towards the howl of the hound in the night. Diarmaid lay down and a deep sleep and a lasting slumber came over him, but the howl of the hound awakened him a third time. And daylight came upon him after that, and he rose up and

said that he would go in the direction of the howl of the hound now that morning had come.

As much inside himself as outside himself, the unintegrated hound had raised the unintegrated boar that would sheath his tusk in his soft groin.

And our lament is for you, Diarmaid dead-bhán, dreach-sholas Ó Duibhne and for you Gráinne inghion Chormaic mhic Airt mhic Cuinn Chéadchathaigh.

In this our lament for you, Gráinne, we remember that you are a daughter of wolf-suckled Cormac son of Bear.

Never again, we believed, would the Beast in us turn on us. Even so, in a time of

Eagla Fhinn

in a time when our soul was the size of our fear of Fionn, of

Fionn and his Hounds

in a time when our soul was the size of current convention, Gráinne led us to

An Braon Beag Baoth-Uisge

In that little drop of unconventional water our unconventional soul is safe.

Not safe in the sense that it cannot be killed. In killing the salmon in the well Cú Chulainn killed Cú Roí.

And that, for sure, is an unconventional sense of things.

To go back into it, no, to go forward into it, following Gráinne, that is the 1916 we need.

Its slogan

Am hé i llind

Ollamh Fódhla would go further saying, that in the deep places of who we are each one of us is

Eó fis i llind

Tat tvam asi

Danu

I

IT WAS nature that shaped them, that moulded them. Given their perfection of form on an Irish horizon, it wouldn't be going too far to say that it was nature itself that sculpted them.

Nature wasn't in a hurry. It had time on its hands. It had long geological epochs and ages to work in. It worked with earth tremors and rivers. It worked with the big and the small rock fracturings of fire and ice. It worked with the erosions and corrosions of wind and rain. And there they are now, two hills, two perfect breasts on a horizon in Ireland. Having cairns for nipples, the old ceo draíochta veils and unveils them.

The Paps, they are called.

The Paps of Danu.

From of old, Danu has been called the mother of the Irish gods. And that's saying something.

That's saying she is mother of Lugh, the Sun God.

That's saying that she is mother of red-mouthed Morrigu, the battle goddess.

That's saying she is mother of Cú Roí mac Daire, the god in a grey mantle who one day picked up his own severed head and walked away.

That's saying she is mother of Midir and Manannán. Manannán is god of the sea, or a god who lives in the sea. Manannán only needs to shake his red and green cloak between his wife and her lover and never afterwards will they so much as remember each other. Never afterwards will they so much as catch sight of each other in a dream.

Being the mother of the Irish gods, Danu is mother of the salmon-god, all-seeing and all-wise in the Boyne, all-wise but blind in Assaroe.

A goddess of the Indo-Europeans, Danu migrated with her people. She migrated with those of them who eventually made it to India, and so it is no surprise to find that there are hymns to her in the Rig Veda. Also of course she migrated with those of her people who came into Europe. On her way west, she gave her name to three rivers, the Dnieper, the Don and the Danube.

And here on a horizon of Ireland's dreamtime are two holy hills, her opulent breasts.

When the mist disperses we see that their nipples are cairns.

II

How do I approach hills so holy? Do I do what his God commanded Moses to do, do I put off my shoes from off my feet?

I don't mean my physical shoes, my physical boots, the boots I bought recently in Stanley's in Clifden.

I mean the cosmologies I'm shod in.

My head shod, my seeing shod, my thinking shod, my talking shod. Shod in touch. In hearing shod.

So shod, I hurt the earth I walk on.

I hear a sheep farmer calling his dog. Whistling like him, calling as echoingly loud and long as he calls, I too should call, calling my cosmologies home from the universe.

Nights there are when I feel that all cosmological thinking about them hurts the stars.

So strangely near some nights are the stars, so like next-door neighbours are they, that I leave my door open, expecting Virgo or Capricorn or Aquarius to drop in.

It would be wrong, wouldn't it, to walk cosmologically roughshod over them?

I will.

I'll put off my shoes from my feet.
I'll put off all cosmologies from my mind.

III

Dien Cecht, the healer among the Tuatha Dé, he came this way.
Singing with it, singing its song of many sounds, he crossed this
stream, leaving a scent not of this world in the heather. Getting
that scent, a hare stopped in his tracks, a low, defunct lobe alive
again.

A scent of Otherworlds. A scent of summer thunder. Coming home one night, Dien Cecht heard a howling, high and far
away. He looked around: its mouth wide open, fiercely fanged
and angry, the lightning struck.

For the very short while that he was on fire, he saw into all
worlds.

In those few moments he was welcome in all worlds.

He heard their songs.

He saw our hurt.

Dien Cecht had no choice. Smelling of thunder, blackened
and singed, his face and his hands peeling like birch bark, he
was now a healer.

While he heals, singing the songs he heard, he is sometimes
an ecstasy of fire, sometimes of ashes.

While he heals a howling, high and far away, is heard.

He came this way.

In his footsteps, picking up the strange scent, I climb.

IV

To be mirrored in the little lake that mirrors the Paps – that is
strange. It is like an invitation into a purer, clearer experience of
ourselves. It is like falling asleep in one world and waking up in
another. It is like falling asleep in Ireland and waking up in Iath
nAnann.

It happens, doesn't it?

An old fiddler leaves a neighbour's house, and he walks towards home, his eyes as he does so getting used to the dark. But he doesn't walk in his own door that night. Not that night. Nor the next night. Not the next night after that.

Sight nor light of him there isn't till nine nights later. Offering no explanation or excuse, he sits by the fire.

He needs time.

He needs to get used to things.

When he is sure of things he goes and takes down his fiddle and he plays the air he heard in the Otherworld.

His wife would hear it all over again.

He hesitates.

'Play it,' she says.

'Such airs', he says, 'must create their own instruments.'

'Such airs', he says, 'must create their own world. A world they can be played in. And hearing they must create. Hearing they can be heard with.'

Tonight, only himself and his wife listening, he plays the air he heard in an immaculate dimension of the world.

V

It isn't yet the tundra I would expect it to be, this high ground between the Paps.

After five or six hours sitting below thin little falls and cascades of water there is something I know. I know that my empirical mind is the third eye's blindspot.

VI

Sometimes it's us who are visionary.

Sometimes it's things.

This evening, here between the Paps, it's this autumn red rowan, red with red berries and a few red leaves.

Even if no one ever laid eyes on it, it would be a vision.

Even in a universe in which eyesight hadn't yet evolved, it would be a vision.

In its presence I'm embarrassed by eyesight. By the little self-serving efficiencies of eyesight.

After three or four hours in its presence I yet again know that there is a rare state of mind that makes my head obsolete.

VII

Climbing steeply, I come up onto a green flood-plain, its grass close cropped by the Pap's sheep.

Looking up at the high horizon round me now, a fear I had setting out deepens into trepidation.

I sit on the fallen wall of an old stone sheep pen.

Remembering another day among other mountains, I don't need to be told that now again I have come up into a height where I am threatened by an avalanche. Not a physical avalanche. Not an avalanche of snow or scree.

At worst, such an avalanche can only overwhelm us downwards into death.

Altogether more frightful is a spiritual avalanche. An avalanche set off by pride, by wilful self-promotion. An avalanche set off by our unreadiness for the heights we have come up into. Such an avalanche can carry us down out of the world altogether. It can carry us down, frightened and alive, into what at first contact will seem to be endless perdition in an endless vacancy.

Also there is an inner apocalypse of insight that leaves us bewildered and desperate, knowing that, conscious and unconscious, psyche is the blind not the window.

Because, I suppose, of its association with sheep pens as forgotten and old as the one I am sitting on, I take refuge in a song called 'Dónal Óg'. It's the young woman who loved and still loves him who sings:

Do gheallais domhsa, ní ba dheacair duit,
loingeas óir faoi chrann seoil airgid
dhá bhaile dhéag de bhailte margaidh
is cúirt bhréa aolta cois taobh na farraige.

Do gheallais domhsa, ní narbh fhéidir,
go dtabharfá laimhne de chroicean eisc dom
go dtabharfá bróga de chroiceann éan dom
is culaith den tsíoda ba dhaoire in Éirinn.

Yes, ships of gold with masts of silver he promised her. Twelve market towns and a house by the sea he promised her. Gloves made by elves and shoes made in fairy forts he promised her. And, altogether more passionately to be desired, he promised that he'd be at the sheep croft waiting for her.

Do gheallais domhsa, agus d'insis bréag dom,
go mbeifeá romhamsa ag cró na gcaorach …

And she would be there. Whatever the weather, she would be there. A bull in a field she must cross, a flood in a river she must ford, three gaps and a fourth gap closed against her, nothing would stop her, she would be there because he would be there, a man of his word, at the sheep croft waiting.

Sheltering from this shower, sheltering at this near gable, he'll surely be, she thought, coming over the brow of the last ridge.

But no! No matter. It's lambing time and he's busy.

Only one more stream to ford, and two rising fields, and then he'll look round, and how glad he will be to see it's me who is there.

But no! Not in the pens.

Not in the near field. Not in the far field.

And the sheep not gathered.

She opens a door.

No. Not inside either.

And not in the hay loft.

Back on the ridge, the better to see, she looks down into the valley. She looks down dumbfounded into a dream dreamed three nights ago. Dónal Óg with his back to her, his belongings slung over his shoulder.

She whistles for Dónal. And she calls. Three hundred times she calls. But a lamb bleating, and he bleating weakly, is all she gets for answer:

Do ligeas fead agus trí cead glaoch chughat
is ni bhfuaireas ann ac uan ag meilig.

Months later, her heart black as a coal on the floor of a forge, she sings, singing to him who isn't there:

Bhainis soir díom is do bhainis siar díom,
Bhainis romham is do bhainis im dhiaidh díom,
Bhainis an gealach is do bhainis an grian díom,
's is ro-mhór m'eagla gur bhainis Dia díom.

You have taken my east from me,
And you have taken my west from me;
You have taken my before-me from me,
And you have taken my behind-me from me;
You have taken the moon and taken the sun from me;
And 'tis my great fear
That you have taken my God from me.

Dónal and Danu.

No sign of Dónal at the sheep croft. And, at the sheep pen here between her own breasts, no sign of Danu.

VIII

Night. Dark night.
Dark night outside.
Dark night inside.
But I praise you, Danu, that you will not condescend to sensory need.

I praise you, Danu, that you will not condescend to apparition.

Here between your breasts it is as absence that you are present.

That, or like Dónal Óg, your back is turned and you are walking away.

The lament of a woman for Dónal could be the lament of a bhakta for Danu:

Tá mo chroíse chomh dubh le hairne
nó le gual dubh a bheadh i gcearta,
nó le bonn bróige ar halla bána
is tá lionn dubh mór os cionn mo gháire.

My heart is as black as the sloe,
as black as a coal that you'd find in a forge,
as black as the track of a shoe in a white hall,
and suffocated by a blackness is my laughter.

And yet there they are, there between your breasts, Danu, are the four elevations of the mystical ascent to which you call us, the elevation of the lake, the elevation of the first flood-plain, the elevation of the second flood-plain and then, veiled by what we see, by vision veiled, the heights.

Often, by frightful but blessed reversal of expectation, it is the avalanche that carries us down into the depths that also carries us into the heights.

It is in an inner apocalypse, an apocalypse of divinely vouchsafed illumination and grace that a way is opened for us.

And so, getting to know you in a way that Hindus didn't know you, in a way that our ancestors in Ireland didn't know you, can we think of you, Danu, as the goddess we only see when your back is turned, as the goddess we only see when you are walking away.

That is your glory. And, even when our heart is as black as a nugget of coal on the floor of a forge, it is our glory.

I praise you, Danu, for not being at our beck and call.

I praise you, Danu, for your beneficent refusal to take up residence in our myths and stories about you.

I praise you, Danu, that you do not attempt to win favour with us by accepting a niche in a religion which, in its ignorance, would shorten the distance between the human and the divine.

And yet, in contradiction to all of this, there they are, two lovely hills in west Munster. They have cairns for nipples. The old ceo draíochta veils and unveils them.

Looking at them, we know how bountifully immanent in all things is the Transcendent Divine. As the breasts of the goddess Danu, it is bountifully immanent in the herb that heals us, in the cancer that kills us.

Having wandered outwards into an illusory sense of existence in independence from the Ground that grounds us, we live and are lived by the contradiction.

For the transcendent way in which you are so mountainously immanent in sand-grain and galaxy, I praise you, Danu.

Of old, in Ireland, they called you.

Bandia an tSonusa
The Goddess of Prosperity.

But you are more, a goddess marvellously more, than your breasts here – below suggest that you are.

You are Danu. Prayed to in India, prayed to in Ireland, who but you can sponsor and propose the Mandukya Upanishad as the meeting ground of East and West, of people praying by Galway Bay and the Bay of Benegal.

You are Danu.

IX

The rowan I remember.

The autumn red rowan growing between two cascades and falls of water.

Even if no one ever laid eyes on it, it would be a vision.

Even in a universe in which eyesight hadn't yet evolved, it would be a vision.

A red Rig Veda in Ireland it is,
A red Gita to Danu in Ireland it is,
A Mandukya dawn over Danu's Ireland it is,
This
Little Yggdrasil

And the berries I picked from the mosses beneath it – closing my hand on them they feel like a rosary.

A rosary of fallen berries.
Of berries fallen from the world tree.

Sometimes they feel like ragnarok.

And in the walk of her, walking to meet him, there were splendours of passionate life.

In the walk of her walking through fair and through field to meet him – in the walk of her walking to meet Dónal Óg, all our contemporary cosmologies were refuted.

As they are in our ascent between your breasts to you, Danu.

There is a rare state of mind in which the empirical mind is blindspot.

And that is a song that Dien Cecht, our divine healer, has yet to learn.

Christk

I T BEGAN in egressus:

Et egressus est Jesus cum discipulis suis trans torrentem Cedron.
And Jesus went forth with his disciples over a torrent called
the Kedron.

And they came to a place which was named Gethsemane:
and he saith to his disciples, Sit ye here, while I shall pray.
And he taketh with him Peter and James and John, and
began to be sore amazed, and to be very heavy.

Sore amazed by what he knows.

What the Psalmist knows, he knows:

I am fearfully and wonderfully made.

What Heraclitus knows, he knows:

You would not find the boundaries of the soul, even by
travelling along every path, so deep a measure does it have.

What Jacob Boehme knows, he knows:

In man is all whatsoever the sun shines upon or heaven
contains, also hell and all the deeps.

What Sir Thomas Browne knows, he knows:

There is all Africa and her prodigies in us.

What William Law knows, he knows:

Thy natural senses cannot possess God or unite thee to Him; nay, thy inward faculties of understanding, will and memory, can only reach after God, but cannot be the place of His habitation in thee. But there is a root or depth in thee whence all these faculties come forth as lines from a centre, or as branches from the body of the tree. This depth is called the centre, the fund or bottom of the soul. This depth is called the unity, the eternity – I had almost said the infinity – of thy soul; for it is so infinite that nothing can satisfy it or give it any rest but the infinity of God.

The time of disputing and speculating upon ideas is short; it can last no longer than whilst the sun of this world can refresh your flesh and blood, and so keep the soul from knowing its own depth or what has been growing in it. But when this is over, then you must know and feel what it is to have a nature as deep and strong and large as eternity.

What William Wordsworth knows, he knows:

Not chaos, not
The darkest pit of lowest Erebus,
Nor aught of blinder vacancy scooped out
By help of dreams – can breed such fear and awe
As fall upon us often when we look
Into our Minds, into the Mind of Man –

What Baudelaire knows, he knows:

Homme libre, toujours tu chériras la mer!
La mer est ton miroir; tu contemples ton âme
Dans le déroulement infini de sa lame
Et ton esprit n'est pas un gouffre moins amer.

What Hopkins knows, he knows:

O the mind, mind has mountains; cliffs of fall
Frightful, sheer, no-man-fathomed ...

What Emerson knows, he knows:

It is the largest part of a man that is not inventoried. He has many enumerable parts: he is social, professional, political, sectarian, literary, in this or that set or corporation. But after the most exhausting census has been made, there remains as much more which no tongue can tell. And this remainder is that which interests.

What Nietzsche discovered, he knows:

I have discovered for myself that the old human and animal life, indeed the entire prehistory and past of all sentient being, works on, loves on, hates on, thinks on in me.

What Conrad knows, he knows:

The mind of man is capable of anything – because everything is in it, all the past as well as all the future.

What William James knows, he knows:

The further limits of our being plunge, it seems to me, into an altogether other dimension of existence from the sensible and the merely understandable.

What D.H. Lawrence knows, he knows:

> There is that other universe, of the heart of man
> that we know nothing of, that we dare not explore.
> A strange grey distance separates
> our pale mind still from the pulsing continent
> of the heart of man.
>
> Fore-runners have barely landed on the shore
> and no man knows, no woman knows
> the mystery of the interior
> when darker still than Congo or Amazon
> flow the heart's rivers of fullness, desire and distress.

What Rilke knows, he knows:

However vast outer space may be, yet with all its sidereal

distances, it hardly bears comparison with the dimension, with the depth dimension of our inner being, which does not even need the spaciousness of the universe to be within itself almost unfathomable.

A Bright Angel Trail of Mahavakyas and to have set deinan-thropic foot on it and to have walked down along it, that already is to have found one's way, as Jesus did, to the floor of the Canyon, that already is to be sore amazed and very heavy, already that is Passion

It is the one, vast, simultaneous adventure of who we phylogenetically and immortally are because as Sir Thomas Browne reminds us:

> There is surely a piece of Divinity in us, something that was before the Elements and owes no homage unto the Sun.

And yes, it is down onto the floor of the Canyon that Jesus has come.

And Bright Angel is there and he points to a mirroring rock-pool and Jesus goes down on His knees and He cups His fin-fraught hands into it and when the water in the cup has settled and it too is mirroring the karma of the ages He drinks it.

A cup of trembling it is and the very lees of it He drinks, and His dread is that what happened to Nebuchadnezzar might happen to Him:

> The same hour was the thing fulfilled upon Nebuchadnezzar: and he was driven from men, and did eat grass as oxen, and his body was wet with the dew of heaven, till his hairs were grown like eagles' feathers, and his nails like birds' claws.

Idumea, in Isaiah's prophetic vision of it, is His dread, His dread that it is a vision of what might happen to His own mind:

> But the cormorant and the bittern shall possess it: the owl also and the raven shall dwell in it: and he shall stretch out upon it the line of confusion, and the stones of emptiness. They shall call the nobles thereof to the kingdom, but none shall be there, and all her princes shall be nothing. And

thorns shall come up in her palaces, nettles and brambles in the fortresses thereof: and it shall be an habitation of dragons, and a court for owls. The wild beasts of the desert shall also meet with the wild beasts of the island, and the satyr shall cry to his fellow; the screech owl also shall rest there, and find for herself a place of rest. There shall the great owl make her nest, and lay, and hatch, and gather under her shadow: there shall the vultures also be gathered, every one with her mate.

And the Psalms speak their passions to Him, speak calamity to Him and hope to Him:

Fearfulness and trembling are come upon me, and horror hath overwhelmed me.

Save me from the lion's mouth: for thou hast heard me from the horns of the unicorns.

Save me, O God; for the waters are come in unto my soul.

Let not the waterflood overflow me, neither let the deep swallow me up, and let not the pit shut her mouth upon me.

I am counted with them that go down into the pit.

Thou hast laid me in the lowest pit, in darkness, in the deeps.

O God, thou hast cast us off, thou hast scattered us, thou hast been displeased; O turn thyself to us again. Thou hast made the earth to tremble; thou hast broken it: heal the breaches thereof for it shaketh. Thou hast shewed thy people hard things: thou hast made us to drink the wine of astonishment.

Therefore will not we fear, though the earth be removed, and though the mountains be carried into the midst of the sea.

Truly my soul waiteth upon God, from him cometh my salvation.

Our heart is not turned back, neither have our steps declined from thy way; Though thou hast sore broken us in the place of dragons, and covered us with the shadow of death.

He brought me up also out of an horrible pit, out of the miry clay, and set my feet upon a rock, and established my goings.

Deep calleth unto deep at the noise of thy waterspouts: all thy waves and thy billows are gone over me.

If I ascend up into heaven, thou art there: if I make my bed in hell, behold, thou art there. If I take the wings of the morning, and dwell in the uttermost parts of the sea; Even there shall thy hand lead me, and thy right hand shall hold me.

And Job – Job He can hear:

For the thing which I greatly feared is come upon me, and that which I was afraid of is come unto me.

My days are past, my purposes are broken off, even the thought of my heart.

His confidence shall be rooted out of his tabernacle, and it shall bring him to the king of terrors.

They came upon me as a wide breaking in of waters: in the desolation they rolled themselves upon me.

Hell is naked before him, and destruction hath no covering.

I am a brother to dragons and a companion to owls.

I have said to corruption, Thou art my father: to the worm, Thou art my mother, and my sister.

Jonah He can hear:

The waters compassed me about, even to the soul: the depth closed me round about, the weeds were wrapped about my head. I went down to the bottoms of the moun-

tains; the earth with her bars was about me forever: yet hast
thou brought up my life from corruption, O Lord my God.

The cup of trembling He drinks.
The wine of astonishment He drinks.

And standing there alone on the Canyon floor, He breathes
Kainozoic air, the same air that lizard and fox and egret and
bighorn and humming bird and owl and moth and butterfly
and squirrel and woodlouse and rattlesnake breathe.

Sinking into Himself, He breathes Mesozoic air, the same
air that ichthyosaurus and tyrannosaurus and styracosaurus and
ornithamimus and meganeura and mischoptera and archaeo-
pteryx breathe.

And gone still farther down into Himself, gone down into
His own embryonic origins, He 'breathes' Palaeozoic 'air', the
same that sponge and jellyfish and crinoid and ammonite and
trilobite and brachiopod breathe.

In Him, as He stands there, the earth in all its geological
ages is psychologically synchronous.

As crinoid He prays.

As styracosaurus He prays.

As bighorn He prays.

Little wonder that our myths of most nerve stop short.

Little wonder that our rituals of most nerve stop short.

Little wonder that Peter, James and John recoil and take
refuge in sleep.

Little wonder that Nietzsche recoils and takes refuge with
Somnus, in quotidian somnambulation.

But Jesus endures.

And, on a presumption of enabling grace, there is further
evolution for us and for all things in watching with Him.

And now, not red, and having a metaphorless look about it,
Good Friday dawns upon us.

And, our myths, even though it is only calamitously that
they can comfort us, they have fallen behind.

And our stories and tall tales, even though it is only with happy or sad endings that they can comfort us, they too have fallen behind.

But, prompted by Christ Himself in a dream, one of the Magi, the only one of them who is still alive, he has come back, and the wisdom-story he tells us pioneers a watching way for us:

No one in living memory had lived the religious life so intensely as Narada had. At an age when all the young men of his village had marriage in mind, he renounced the world and retired to a forest, practising austerities so damaging to life and limb they would soon have killed a lesser man. Over the years there was no obstruction, no matter how integral to his worldly identity, that he didn't take on. In the end, even Vishnu, the Great God himself, marvelled at his hunger and thirst, killing ordinary hunger and thirst, for final liberation and so it was that he did something he never before did.

Coming down out of his high heaven, he stood in Narada's door, telling him that he would grant him any boon he desired. All he had to do was name it.

'To know the secret of your Maya,' Narada replied.

Vishnu smiled discouragingly.

Fierce in all his undertakings and ways, Narada persisted.

'Very well then,' Vishnu said, 'we will walk together, you and I.'

It was a long trudge through the forest and then, Vishnu complaining already of tiredness, they trudged through difficult scrubland.

They came into a red desert. So fierce was the sun, it didn't only boil their blood, it boiled their minds. Coming to a great rock and unable to put one buckling leg past the other, Vishnu sat down in its shallow shade, saying, 'Here I stay, here I die, unless, of course, you find and bring me water, how soon you can see for yourself.'

Narada set off.

The only thing in him that didn't crack was his will.

He saw a green haze on the horizon.

And no, looking at it, he concluded that it wasn't a mirage. Indeed, now with every excited step of the way, it looked more real, and soon he was walking in the cool of great green trees. He knocked on the first door he came to.

So instantly bewitched was he by the charm of the young woman who opened the door to him that he altogether forgot Vishnu and his distress. Utterly charmed, he walked in and sat down, neither he nor they of the house making strange with each other.

He ate an evening meal with them.

Next morning he went to work in their fields with them.

That's how it was for two whole years.

Alone with him one day, Narada asked the man of the house for the hand of his daughter in marriage.

It was a joyous wedding.

A child, a boy, was born to them. Then a girl and again a girl.

Seven years later, the monsoon clouds were like oceans hanging above the world and they hadn't far to fall and they all seemed to fall together and within a few hours. Chaos swirling and roaring everywhere, Narada and his family were out of doors seeking the safety of higher ground. First one child, then another was swept away. The old man and the old woman were tumbled beneath a tumbling dyke. Then Narada himself was engulfed and carried ten times down into ten ever deeper drownings, only he didn't drown, couldn't drown, and then, like waking from a dream or like waking from waking it was, he was walking, his brain boiled, in a red desert, and all around him, everywhere yet nowhere, he heard it, the voice of the Great God asking, 'You've been gone for almost an hour, did you bring the water?'

The question that would turn any day into Good Friday.

Good Friday. Dis-illusioning day. Day we come to see that just as Narada walked into the green haze so, having walked into it, are we bewitched by the world. Only now, having undergone his dis-illusioning with Narada, we talk, not about the world, but about the world-mirage, we talk about the world-illusion.

'And what,' we asked the Magus, 'what is the source of the world-illusion? How or where or in what does it arise?'

Judging us able for it, he tells us another story:

A man is walking home late one evening. Having worked all day under the burning sun, he is looking forward to the cool of his house, to food and rest. Suddenly he sees a snake, coiled and ready to strike, on the side of the road. Reacting in terror, he leaps aside, aside and again aside. At a safe distance, he opens his eyes and to his great relief he sees, not a snake, but a coil of rope fallen most likely from an ox cart trudging on ahead of him.

Out of our own minds the snake-illusion, the world-illusion, we say.

'But', says the Magus, 'to know that is not yet to have won liberation. It isn't only Hindu traders who come to our land. Buddhist traders come, and a story they tell is our story too:

A prince by birth he was, a prince from a far away land, but after ten years with the world's greatest master in the arts of offence and defence he was called Prince Five Weapons, that in open recognition of his prowess in these same arts.

Everyone sad to see him go, he set out for home.

He came to a forest.

People who lived within sight of it warned him saying, that if he valued his life he wouldn't so much as think of entering it because that, even that, would arouse the wrath of the Ogre, called Sticky Hair, who lived in it.

Nothing daunted, Prince Five Weapons continued on his way, on and on, till he heard the roar that felled every tree between him and … whatever he was – a hundred shapes at once he was. Prince Five Weapons entertained himself with his small-eyed rhinoceros charge and with his wide-horned, wide-nostrilled buffalo charge, with his invisible tiger stalk, with his open-jawed lion-leap into the tusked Ogre, huge and sticky-haired, enjoying one of those rare times when he could live with himself without having to endure the horror of being himself.

Sure of his aim, Prince Five Weapons launched his spear, its head hungry for murder. For all the perfection of its flight, it shuddered and stopped dead in the Ogre's sticky hair.

Stretching a bow half as tall as himself, he released an arrow, it's head sleek with deadly venom. Reaching its target, it whirred and stopped dead, stuck in the sticky hair.

Closing upon him in a sequence of disconcerting sleights of movement, he struck with his sword. It stuck to him.

Charging him with it, his dagger stuck to him. Bringing it down upon him, his club stuck to him. He hit him with his right fist. It stuck to him. He hit him with his left fist. It stuck to him. He pounded him with his head. It stuck to him. He kicked him with his right foot. It stuck to him. He kicked him with his left foot. It stuck to him.

What surprised and then enraged the Ogre was that even now, ripe though he was for devouring, Prince Five Weapons showed no fear.

'Why aren't you trembling?' Sticky Hair raged. 'Why, like every one else who has dared to come this way, are you not pleading for your wretched little life?'

''Tis you should be trembling,' Prince Five Weapons said.

Shocked at first, the monster recovered and roared a buffalo roar, in huge, disbelieving derision.

'Roar as you will,' said Prince Five Weapons, 'but not all of me is stuck to you, within me is eternal diamond life and if you swallow me it will shatter you as a thunderbolt would.'

Astonished and fearing for himself, Sticky Hair trembled and, his devouring power over him at an end, Prince Five Weapons walked free.

Having given us a long time to reflect on how sticky the world might be and on how stuck to it we might be, it mattering but little whether that world is real or illusory, for to be stuck to a figment is as disabling as to be stuck to a fact – having given us Good Friday time to reflect on all of this, he told us that Prince Five Weapons was the Buddha in an earlier incarnation.

And he chanted for us the Buddha's Udana, the great and to us terrible words that he spoke on the morning of his enlightenment as he sat in the lotus position, touching the earth, requesting it to bear witness:

> Through many rounds
> From birth to death have I
> Toiled, seeking but not finding
> The builder of the house.
>
> House-builder, I behold you now;
> Again a house you will not build.
> All your rafters are broken now,
> The ridgepole also is thrown down:
> My mind, its elements dissolved,
> The end of craving has attained.

It is Good Friday, somewhere between the sixth and the ninth hour. It is like waking up, but not into waking. It is like waking up into dreamless sleep, into the no-thing-ness of dreamless sleep or into something beyond it that we have no name for.

Asking us to look up with our extinguished eyes and minds to the terrible summit, the Magus somehow gives us to know that it is to the crossed ridgepole and rafter of overthrown selfhood that Jesus is pinned back, and it is from here, His head falling forward onto His chest, that He looks down into the anasravic skull, His own and Adam's.

And now, still in baptismal assimilation to Him, it remains to us to abide in the dark, it remains to us to be as out of God's way awake as we are in dreamless sleep.

And, down the centuries, many are they who have so abided, and many are they to whom God has been eternally gracious.

To Eckhart eternally gracious:

Comes then the soul into the unclouded light of God. It is transported so far from creature-hood into nothingness that, of its own powers, it can never return to its agents or its former creaturehood. Once there, God shelters the soul's nothingness with his uncreated essence, safeguarding its creaturely existence. The soul has dared to become nothing, and cannot pass from its own being into nothingness and then back again, losing its own identity in the process, except God safeguarded it. This must needs be so.

Oh, wonder of wonders, when I think of the union the soul has with God! He makes the enraptured soul to flee out of herself, for she is no more satisfied with anything that can be named. The spring of Divine Love flows out of the soul and draws her out of herself into the unnamed Being, into her first source, which is God alone.

To Marguerite Porete, God was eternally gracious:

Being completely free, and in command on her sea of peace, the soul is nonetheless drowned and loses herself through God, with him and in him. She loses her identity, as does the water from a river – like the Ouse or the Meuse – when it flows into the sea. It has done its work and can relax in the arms of the sea, and the same is true of the soul. Her work is over and she can lose herself in what she has totally become: Love. Love is the bridegroom of her happiness enveloping her wholly in his love and making her part of that which is. This is a wonder to her and she has become a wonder. Love is her only delight and pleasure.

The soul now has no name but Union in Love. As the

water that flows into the sea becomes sea, so does the soul become Love. Love and the soul are no longer two things but one. She is then ready for the next stage.

Reason: Can there be a next stage after this?

Love: Yes, once she has become totally free, she then falls into a trance of nothingness, and this is the next highest stage. There she no longer lives in the life of grace, nor in the life of the spirit, but in the glorious life of divinity. God has conferred this special favour on her and nothing except his goodness can now touch her …What it means is being in God without being oneself, since to be in God is being …

To Henry Suso, God was eternally gracious:

When the good and faithful servant enters into the joy of his Lord, he is inebriated by the riches of the house of God; for he feels, in an ineffable degree, that which is felt by the inebriated man. He forgets himself, he is no longer conscious of his selfhood; he disappears and loses himself in God, and becomes one spirit with him, as a drop of water which is drowned in a great quantity of wine. For even as such a drop disappears, taking the colour and taste of wine, so it is with those who are in full possession of blessedness …

Epilogue:
Overcoming Our Serglige

A LONG TIME ago, in Ireland, Cú Chulainn, the national hero, succumbed to serglige, to a wasting sickness. No one, including Cú Chulainn himself, knowing the real cause, people were free to adduce all kinds of spurious causes, none more so than the one that caught on, this having it that, in consequence of adultery across a praeternatural border, he had been whipped by three women from the Otherworld.

Free to speculate then, we are free to speculate now.

Could it be that, having outgrown him, people were withdrawing their imaginative support of him from him? A hero who has drawn his energy from such support and who now finds that it is no longer forthcoming will almost certainly waste away, pine away, fade away, as Cú Chulainn in fact did.

Or, could it be that we have got it the wrong way round? Could it be that it was the people who first succumbed to serglige, their imagination so wasting that they could no longer either conceive or credit a hero? Did the wasting simultaneously afflict the one and the other, laying a people and their hero low? Is it the case that whatever afflicts a hero afflicts his people? Are we talking about a people in decline? Then and now? The fact that we nowadays seem to be content with such heroes as the Playboy of the Western World and Leopold Bloom, is that a symptom of serglige? And Yeats, what of him? Surely, the only thing about Cú Chulainn that should have interested him was his wasting. His wasting and our wasting. More creatively, he might have concerned himself with the transition from one hero to another, from Cú Chulainn to Christ. Being an utterly new kind of hero, Jesus pioneered and validated and inaugurated a new kind of heroism. But now that Jesus in turn is undergoing a wasting, a fading from the cultural scene, this maybe is a good time to remember Him, for it could be that, in spite of our claim to the contrary, we are wasting with Him.

From the moment He crossed the Torrent into a karmic profundity of the earth called Gethsemane, Jesus was a hero not of anthropic but of deinanthropic humanity. This, perhaps, calls for comment.

In the early decades of the nineteenth century people we would now think of as palaeontologists began to look at fossils in a new and more rigorously scientific way. Above all else they set about the work of classifying them, assigning them to phyla, genera and species, this preparatory to the not so onerous business of naming them. It fell to Owen of the Natural History Museum in London to name an extinct lizard of gigantic proportions. Adding not just to the scientific but to the popular lexicon, he combined the Greek word 'deinos', meaning terrible, with the Greek word 'saurus' meaning lizard, and trimmed the resulting compound to 'dinosaur'.

Of course, the Greek word 'deinos' doesn't only mean terrible. It can, all at once, mean uncanny, strange, inordinate, having what makes it a wonder, that and more. And so, when we combine this word, meaning all that it does, with another Greek word, 'anthropus', meaning the human in an essential and generic sense, we get the noun 'deinanthropus' and the adjective 'deinanthropic', the implication being that we ourselves are everything the qualifying word means, inordinate, uncanny, strange, terrible in the old Latin sense of the word 'terribilis', a wonder, that and more.

The Psalmist had a truly deinanthropic sense of us when he said:

I am fearfully and wonderfully made.

As did Jacob Boehme when he said:

In man is all whatsoever the sun shines upon or heaven contains, also hell and all the deeps.

In other words, we aren't only a microcosm, the universe in little. In us also are such transcosmic immensities as heaven and hell, and the deeps as well, all of them.

Hopkins tells us that we are unfathomable to ourselves:

O the mind, mind has mountains; cliffs of fall
Frightful, sheer, no-man-fathomed. Hold them cheap
May who ne'er hung there …

When Conrad says that:

The mind of man is capable of anything, because everything is in it, all the past as well as all the future.

he is talking about who and what we phylogenetically have been, are, and will be, that being only a portion of who and what we deinanthropically are. Nevertheless, it is no small matter to discover as Nietzsche did that what we have been down the evolutionary ages is still active in us:

I have discovered for myself that the old human and animal life, indeed the entire prehistory and past of all sentient being, works on, loves on, hates on, thinks on, in me.

Roll away our tidy town park and under it we will find a Jurassic savannah. Roll away the recent overlay in what we sometimes think of as our fully human brain and under it, still active, we will find the reptile brain and the earliest mammalian smell-brain, this the justification for the theronthropic in Greek myth, for Centaur and Minotaur in it.

D.H. Lawrence, however, is either forgetting or ignoring something, or maybe it is that there is something he doesn't know, when he says that we haven't yet ascended our inner Amazon or Congo:

There is that other universe, of the heart of man
that we know nothing of, that we dare not explore.
A strange grey distance separates
our pale mind still from the pulsing continent
of the heart of man.

Fore-runners have barely landed on the shore
and no man knows, no woman knows
the mystery of the interior
when darker still than Congo or Amazon
flow the hearts' rivers of fullness, desire and distress.

The fact is, someone has dared. Jesus has dared to ascend
not just the dark rivers of the heart. Gone down into the underworld of our mind, He has ascended the River of the White
Hippopotamus. In crossing the Torrent, He crossed into all that
we deinanthropically are, not to look around and take stock, but
to live all of it back into God. We can be sure of it, nothing of
what we are, nothing of what is, has been left behind in an outer
darkness. In the final disposition of things there will be no
perdition.

Jesus is the hero of total human in-habitation. He in-habited
us downwards into and upwards from Divine Ground within us.

The news out of Gethsemane and down from Golgotha is
that we have been lived successfully, therefore we are a success,
therefore we can be a success. Be it said of course that it is only
in and with divine assistance that we can be a success. Christians
believe in a god who is willing to be implicated. Who, indeed,
is willing to hang for humanity, and for all things, living and
extinct. Not therefore extinct.

> *Ecce homo*
> *Ecce deinanthropus*

In Christ we see it. It isn't only that we are anthropically
successful. Or, as Chiron was, it isn't only that we are theran-
thropically successful. Christian good news has it that we are
deinanthropically successful. That we didn't hear, climbing be-

tween her breasts, from Danu. That we didn't hear from Manannán singing his Song of God to us at sea. That we didn't hear from headless Cú Roí. But that is no reason why we should forget or ignore these great pagan divinities. Still less is it a reason to banish them to hell as Milton sought to do in his 'Hymn on the Morning of Christ's Nativity'. What is so terrible about polytheistic credence so long as we know that behind the gods and the worlds that emanate from it is the eternal divine One who is One only without a second? Danu showing her breasts, Manannán singing at sea and Cú Roí walking headlessly yet unerringly south through Ireland are immense theophanies, are immense revelations, persuading us surely to go not for a break but for continuity with our pagan past. Continuity not scission is an instinct with the endlessly remembering Irish, is it not? Hence the recurring effort to bring Oisín and Patrick together, in agon, in acallamh or, altogether more amiably, in a dindsenchus walkabout.

And so, to Ireland being one of the ultimate islands of the world. Ultimate geographically, it challenges us, does it not, to be ultimate philosophically and spiritually? At the very least we should live remembering that a strange and very great god called Manannán god of the sea sang a gita at sea to us and that Cú Roí mac Daire, he also a strange and very great god, enacted an Upanishad among us.

A gita like none other in ultimate challenge we have and, challenging us also to ultimate purpose, an Upanishad like none other in dramatic enactment we have.

Think of a holy night in Ireland. Think of the night Manannán walked across the land, across river and mountain and bog, to lie with Caointigirn, his most passionate gopi, his most passionate bhakta, his Irish Radha. Audibly in everything all night long, audibly in rock and bush, in lake-mirrored stars and in the stars themselves, audibly in seeing and in knowing, in instinct audibly, was the singing of the silver branch. And this, we know, is how it is every night in Ireland. This, we know, is how it is in everything everywhere, always. Tonight was every night, ordinary, not miraculous. How things are.

Cú Roí and Cú Chulainn.

Manannán and Caointigirn.

Crunncú and Macha.

Think of the night that Crunncú, her bhakta, had generative sex with Macha the horse goddess.

Think of that neighing night.

Stabled or in the wild, every horse in Ireland neighed that night.

And the night that Macha foaled, that night too they neighed.

Manannán's son by Caointigirn.

Macha's daughter by Crunncú.

Depending on how you are, sight of either of them could mean serglige or healing from serglige.

Although he waited and waited, seeking mediation, Crunncú who heard the hooves of the horse goddess in his yard never once heard the hooves of their daughter in his yard.

It was blindly or, at best, it was unconsciously that Crunncú foresaw his own voidance:

> Attempt to bridle Macha as you'd attempt to bridle an ordinary horse, attempt it, just that, and your face will fall in, into nothingness, into emptiness, into your own empty skull looking back at you as a bridle hanging on a stable wall would.

Hearing the horse goddess he sacrilegiously called Nag neighing from the hills, Crunncú's whole nature fell in.

Cometh the hour, cometh Cú Roí: his head an unnecessary adjunct thrown over his shoulder together with his beheading block and his axe, but there he is, walking unerringly south to his cloud-high house in west Munster. The day we moved from metaphysics to metanoesis, that too was a holy day in Ireland.

It is in metanoesis and ultimately in self-abeyance that we climb to Cú Roí. It is as bhaktas, in passionate devotion to her, that we climb between her breasts to Danu.

In appearance at least, things wholly unlike each other are

those two savage, jagged rocks at sea called Scelec and, inland, those two lovely, rounded hills called Dá Chích Danann.

But then, cut off for months maybe, never ever did the monks who lived on Scelec want for altar wine. Every morning when they went out they would find what they needed in the hollow of a stone outside their oratory. 'Twas as if, for all their savagery and jaggedness, those precipices at sea were the breasts of an androgynous Christ, monks living on the one, sea-birds on the other, and who can say what nurture those sea-birds derive from their *petra fertilis*, from their jagged and savage but fertile rock. Standing on it, do they in unknowing know in their webbed feet that matter is mantra? Could it be that what we first heard from Manannán they hear from their rock, a sea rock white with their droppings? As with them so with us, it is something we mostly aren't aware of that keeps us going. Scelec of the monks proves how right the Psalmist was when he said:

I am fearfully and wonderfully made.

Had he looked across at it from the mainland, Blake might well have asked:

Did he who made Tyger make man?

Altogether more marvellously and sensuously sumptuous, some days, are Dá Chích Danann. Not that their sumptuousness is the whole story. For one thing, the nipples of these divine breasts are cairns, they are tombs, suggesting that even while we are undergoing the disintegrations of death we are for all that being divinely nurtured. What an outcome to a life, to be buried in the tomb-nipples, in the sepulchral nipples, of a great goddess! And the lovely rowan that grows from the moss-covered, heather-covered low rock wall between the breasts themselves. And then, as you climb, you come up onto a green, close-cropped flood-plain that has some old drystone sheep pens on it, over to the right of a gurgling stream. Down from the ravishing heights it comes, that clear stream, and as you drink from it you know that here also is Ireland, ultimately.

Mostly, it is in bhakta yoga that we ascend to Danu. Mostly, it is in jnana yoga that we ascend to Cú Roí. Only, of course, in the course of a single day, the one can graduate into the other and back again, charming us to rapture or to devastation. Here, so terrible is our yearning, we look up and we say or we hear ourselves saying, 'I am willing to leave myself behind in order to get to you, God.' And yes, that finally is what we do, we go on, consciously without ourselves, as we go on, unconsciously without ourselves, in dreamless sleep.

Don't shortchange me with an experience of you, God.

Please, God, be merciful to me, don't shortchange me with an experience of you or, worse still, with a vision of you.

This time immersion beyond dualizing consciousness in the One, who is one only, without a second.

And there it breaks, a Mandukya dawn over Manannán walking out of Caointigirn's door, over Dá Chích Danann, over Cathair Chonroí and, farther west in the sea, over Scelec.

Scelec means Christ and Christ means our graduation from anthropus to deinanthropus and, if personal catastrophe is to be avoided, this must in turn mean our further graduation with God's help back into God.

Only people who haven't yet graduated from anthropus into deinanthropus are in the not entirely enviable position of attempting to make do without God.

Speaking of our no-man-fathomed, inner immensities, Hopkins says:

> Hold them cheap
> May who ne'er hung there ...

Acutely aware of all that distracts us from knowing who we are, William Law will have us know that:

> The time of disputing and speculating upon ideas is short;
> it can last no longer than whilst the sun of this world can

refresh your flesh and blood, and so keep the soul from knowing its own depth or what has been growing in it. But when this is over, then you must know and feel what it is to have a nature as deep and strong and large as eternity.

Having a mostly anthropic, not a deinanthropic, sense of Him, the Gospels are at a loss either to fully estimate or explain the anguish of Jesus in Gethsemane. While an anthropic sense of Him is adequate to what He was and to what He underwent in the Garden of Olives it isn't at all adequate to what He was and to what He underwent in Gethsemane. Also, while an anthropic sense of Him is adequate to what He was and to what He underwent on Calvary, it isn't at all adequate to what He was and to what He underwent on Golgotha. Similarly with regard to Easter morning in the Garden of the Sepulchre and to Easter morning on the shore of the Divine Ungrund.

For the reason that in Him humanity has successfully graduated from anthropus to deinanthropus, Jesus is the best hope we have of a human future.

To be successful, deinanthropus must mean immensities of reliance upon God. Two such immensities we know of, in Gethsemane and on Golgotha.

It is deinanthropically that Gethsemane and Golgotha make sense.

It is deinanthropically that it makes sense to reach for the karmic cup in Gethsemane and to look down into one's own empty skull on Golgotha.

The news of Jesus that St Patrick came to Ireland with isn't the whole story.

Much as Oisín has a long way to go in his Paganism so has St Patrick a long way to go in his Christianity.

Here in Ireland, deepest Paganism and deepest Christianity can enrich each other to unity of vision, to unity of voice.

Blake believed that the antiquities of every other people are as holy as those of the Jews. And Yeats did give some thought to the idea of Christ posed against a background of Celtic myth.

And so, having Cathair Chonroí and Puck Fair in between them, maybe Scelec and Dá Chích Danann can look to each other. For all its savagery, Scelec is a breast that has the wine of salvation in it and it would be folly not to anticipate a no-man-fathomed precipitousness between the breasts of Danu. Even to her most fervent bhakta, Dá Chích Danann will sometimes seem to be Dá Chích na Morrígna. If you doubt it, ask Ollamh Fódhla.

Apart from the challenge of Ireland as a whole think of how much challenge there is in Kerry alone: the challenge of Scelec, that a challenge to sing and live the Beatitudes between the hooked head and the hooked feet of the hawk; the challenge of Cathair Chonroí, that a challenge to be honest with ourselves and with God; the challenge of Dá Chích Danann, this a challenge to acknowledge and accept that as well as a murdering there is a mothering in things.

Hard to say of course whether the mothering is in things as things or whether it is in them from beyond them.

Are the Paps a physics or a metaphysics? Do they testify to metaphysical but not also to physical reality?

Both ways, or either way, they assure us that we are as divinely well nurtured in death as we are in life, and this surely should challenge us to do better than we have been doing. Yet more: it should challenge us to be other than we have been.

The truth is, there are days so gentle, you look up at them and you think, now, everywhere always in all things, the Paps are both metaphysics and physics.

Other days it is Scelec: like the fins of basking sharks closing in for their mouthfuls, it is they in their conscienceless savagery that are the metaphysics and physics of all things.

Pascal wagered on the existence of God but not also on the kind of God God might be, more like Coatlicue than Danu, more like Huitzilopochtli than Lugh, more like Tezcatlipoca than Manannán, more like Xipe Totec than Aengus Óg? A god requiring the Aztec fistful, some days in tens, some days in hundreds, in thousands over a week of rededicating days?

Does the metaphysical have the same hooked head and hooked feet that the hawk does?

The Paps say no.

And Eckhart who had immediate experience of it says no:

> Oh wonder of wonders, when I think of the union the soul has with God! He makes the enraptured soul flee out of herself, for she is no more satisfied with anything that can be named. The spring of Divine Love flows out of the soul and draws her out of herself into the unnamed Being, into her first source, which is God alone.

Vindicating the Paps. Vindicating Scelec wine.

To the extent that we foster it and give into it, our serglige is a disgrace.

How can we be happy that our national eye is a Balar's eye? How can we be happy that our national tongue is a Bricriu's Nemtenga? In Irish a Nemtenga. In English a Nemtenga.

How come that Manannán's Gita-at-Sea isn't our national anthem? How come that the silver branch isn't blazon to our national flag, silver on purple?

Sea mists opening and closing about his high Asgard and he being the god who survives gotterdammerungs, how come that Cú Roí isn't better known? In him is a challenge to ultimacy, philosophical and spiritual. To acknowledge him is to return to a time before the Battle of the Boyne when Ireland belonged to Asia. Asia of the Mandukya Upanishad. Asia of the Tao Te Ching. Asia of the Heart Sutra.

Our new Battle of the Boyne is our aspiration to acquire and live by the insights that Ollamh Fódhla lives by:

> Sensing my difficulties, my father was blunt: if in the eyes of the world you aren't embarrassed by your beliefs about the world then you may conclude that the wonder-eye that is in all of us hasn't yet opened in you.

Dá Chích Danann
Dá Chích na Morrígna

The Paps of Danu
The Paps of Morrigu
The Paps of the goddess as Mother Goddess and the Paps of the goddess as Battle Goddess.

Living in the high summer grazing ground between the Paps of Morrigu Ollamh Fódhla learned that in being religious he must have no recourse to religion. Living in the high summer grazing ground between the Paps of Danu we learn to sing as a bhakta abandoned by her Ishtadevata would sing:

> You have taken my east from me,
> And you have taken my west from me;
> You have taken what was before me from me,
> And you have taken what was behind me from me;
> You have taken the moon from me,
> And you have taken the sun from me,
> And 'tis my great fear that you have taken my god from me.

Call aloud to your goddess or god in such a high place, call out loud up here to Cú Roí or Danu, and you could set off a spiritual avalanche that will carry you all the way down out of an anthropic into a deinanthropic awareness of yourself, and now you are in trouble in the way that no character in Greek tragedy is, in the way that no character in Roman tragedy is, in a way that no character in English Elizabethan and Jacobean tragedy is, in a way that no character in French neoclassical tragedy is. In its entirety now, European literature can only be a Simple Simon to you:

> Simple Simon went a-fishing
> For to catch a whale,
> But all the water he had got
> Was in his mother's pail.

How anthropologically hospitable can the monastery at Saighir be to you now? How anthropologically hospitable can the monastery on Scelec be to you now? Sail out seeking refuge on Scelec now and it is a hailshower of pterosaurs that will be diving into the sea all about you and, arrogantly good though they were at this kind of thing, even Greeks will hesitate to sublimate this Cretaceous Constellation of Kills into our night sky.

Saighir and Scelec, the one the failed hope of the other and you deinanthropically out-of-doors to inhabitable anthropology.

Out-of-doors to Greek myth.
Out-of-doors to Celtic myth.
Out-of-doors to folktale.
Out-of-doors to European literature.
Out-of-doors to all civic logos about anthropus.
Out-of-doors to the history of European philosophy.

Out-of-doors to our Musée de l'Homme.
Out-of-doors to cultured and culturable humanity.

Now it isn't the wedding guest you stop.

Now, having travelled farther than him, it is the Ancient Mariner you stop.

And if Ishmael should come up the road towards you, him you will stop, and to him you will say, only God as Divine Ungrund grounds you.

Now, neither by a conscious resumption of habit nor by deliberate decision, we believe in a god beyond all tales told, beyond all logos about theos.

If you are a Pagan, you have good reason now to fall in with Cú Roí walking south by west through whatever land you happen to be living in.

If you are a Christian, you have good reason now to cross the Torrent with Christ and it won't be an offence to your sense of your individual dignity to do so in sacramental assimilation to Him.

In such assimilation is the ultimate adventure. In nothing else is there anything like it for enormities of night and day, for enormities neither of night nor of day.

Cú Roí and Christ.

If nothing else, Cú Roí walking metanoetically south through Ireland should prepare us for what from the beginning has been the case, the full deinanthropic story:

> In man is all whatsoever the sun shines upon or heaven
> contains, also hell and all the deeps.

Think of an ego trying to direct and control and choreograph
all this.

Inwardly it is something we aren't aware of, not something
we are aware of that supports and sustains us. That something
that we do not know, that we cannot know, in dualizing consciousness – Hindus call it atman Brahman, and, particularly
when we have been cataclysmed out of an anthropic into a
deinanthropic awareness of ourselves it is at once both wise and
desperately expedient to rely on it, not on the ego now more
embarrassingly impotent than ever.

Since the Divine as the One transcends the inside-outside
divide, it matters little whether we think of ourselves turning
inwards towards it or ascending outside ourselves towards it. All
such directions belong to the seeker not to the Sought.

Yeats said that until the Battle of the Boyne Ireland belonged to
Asia, and in translating the greatest of the Upanishads he was no
doubt seeking to bridge the breach, this meaning that in the literal sense of the word he would be pontifex.

And yes, there are hymns to Danu in the Rig Veda, Manannán is the kind of god we might have met out at sea off Cape
Comorin, Cú Roí walking metanoetically south through India
wouldn't seem outlandish, and the pity is that the Christ who
crossed the Torrent, who reached for the karmic cup, who
looked down into His own empty skull, isn't more widely welcome in Asia.

We welcomed Him widely in Ireland, but even on Scelec
you would be tempted to think that we did so superficially. We
welcomed Him as the one who crossed the Kedron, a dried out
wadi, into the Garden of Olives and onwards to Calvary and the
Garden of the Sepulchre not also as the one who crossed the
Torrent into Gethsemane and onwards to Golgotha and the

shore of the Divine Ungrund. The Divine Ungrund that grounds.

To welcome the Christ who crossed the Torrent is to welcome our further and final evolution.

To greet Christ who crossed the Torrent is to greet

GAIAKHTY

It is to greet

BUDDH GAIA

It is for us and for our gods and our heroes to grow with Christ, here in

Irlandia Ultima

here in

Ireland, ultimately

But there could be something in it for Jesus were he to ascend between the Breasts of Danu.

As there could be, were he to do likewise, for Lugh.
As there could be, were she to do likewise, for Macha.
As there could be, were he to do likewise, for Cú Roí.
As there could be, were they to do likewise, for Manannán and Crom Dubh.
As there could be, were she to do likewise, for Danu herself.

We are talking about the most blessed of gotterdammerungs, the return of everything to God as Divine Ungrund, the Divine Ungrund that grounds, and who now, having gone beyond, could ever again settle for rapture, for the vulgarity, by comparison, of rapture, for the vulgarity, by comparison, of bliss.

Shantih　　　　*Shantih*　　　　*Shantih*

Glossary

Acallamh: Literally, 'colloquy' – a talking together.

Aillwee Cave: A long cave in the Burren, County Clare, in which, under a ledge, is a bears' den or place of hibernation.

Am hé i llind: 'I am a salmon in a pool', from Amhairghin Glúngheal's song.

Am séig i n-aill: 'I am a hawk on a cliff', from Amhairghin Glúngheal's song.

Amhairghin Glúngheal: The great poet of the invading Celts.

Asgard: In Norse mythology, the home of Odin, the supreme god and of his warrior offspring, the Aesir.

At-chíu: Literally, 'I see'.

Atman: 'Soul' in Sanscrit.

Balar: In Celtic mythology, the god of death and the king of the Fomorians. He was the son of Buarainech and husband of Cethlenn.

Balar's evil eye: Already of gigantic size and tyrannical in temperament, Balar one day walked past a house in which some druids were brewing the most terrible of poisons in a cauldron. Emerging through a window, the steam from the cauldron infected one of Balar's eyes, and so destructive of the world around it did the eye become that it had to be covered with a nine-layered lid. Here it is the modern economic eye. Its lid lifted from it in the seventeenth century, it is destroying our planet. In all ways it is the opposite of silver-branch perception, which Mannanán mac Lir, the god of the sea, sent ashore and came ashore with.

Banbha: The goddess of Irish sovereignty and of the land of Ireland in one of her three distinct manifestations. Here she represents a distinct dimension of the land of Ireland. See *Éire* and *Fódhla*.

Bealtaine: The month of May or, in particular, May Day.

Bhagavad Gita: The best loved of Hindu religious texts. Spoken by Lord Krishna to Arjuna immediately prior to the Battle of Kurukshetra. Literally, 'Song of God'.

Bhakta: In Hinduism, a passionate devotee of a particular goddess or god.

Bid saineamail ind énflaith: 'The Birdreign is distinguished, is excellent.'

Bindu: The point of universal emergence and return in a mandala.

Birdreign: See *Énflaith*.

Boann: The river Boyne conceived of as a goddess.

Bran mac Feabhail: The hero who met the god Manannán at sea.

Brí Leith: A hill in County Longford traditionally thought to be the home of the god Midir.

Bricriu: A poison-tongued hero of Irish myth.

Bright Angel Trail: One of the winding trails that leads down to the floor of the Grand Canyon in Arizona.

Caointigirn: Manannán's supreme bhakta (*q.v.*) in Ireland, the one he came ashore to lie with and on whom he fathered Morigán.

Caves of Keshcorran, The: Seventeen caves in a limestone cliff on Keshcorran Moutain, County Sligo. It is said that Corran, the harper of the Tuatha Dé Danann, lived in them.

Ceo draíochta: Literally, 'magic mist'. Usually it descends upon someone about to cross over into the Otherworld.

Cnoc Áine and Cnoc Gréne: Hills in County Limerick.

Coatlicue: The Aztec earth goddess.

Colonus Wood: The wood in Attica where Oedipus Rex undergoes final translation into the heavens.

Conaire Mór: The king whose reign in Ireland is known as the Birdreign.

Connla's Well: A name for the Otherworld Well in which the rivers of Ireland were thought to have their source.

Cormac mac Airt: A high king of Ireland in whom Fír Flathemon was supremely well exemplified. See *Fír Flathemon*.

Cruachan: In County Roscommon, the royal centre of the province of Connaught.

Cú Chulainn: Famous Ulster warrior who single-handedly defended the province of Ulster against Queen Medhbh's invading armies.

Cú Roí mac Daire: Euhemerized, he was thought of as a king of west Munster. Here we seek to reimagine him as the god in a grey mantle.

Dá Chích Danann: Two small hills in east Kerry, thought of as the breasts, or paps, of Danu, the divine mother of the Irish gods. See *Paps of Danu*.

Dá Chích na Morrígna: Two small hills in County Meath, thought of as the breasts, or paps, of Morrigu, the war goddess. See *Paps of Morrigu*.

Daedalus: In Greek myth, the greatest and cleverest of craftsmen, and as such an archetype adopted by James Joyce in his role as literary craftsman or artificer.

Deinanthropus: A compound of two Greek words, 'deinos' and 'anthropus', suggesting the inner immensities of the human, as when Jacob Boehme says, 'In man is all whatsoever the sun shines upon or heaven contains, also hell and all the deeps.'

Dergruathar: Literally, 'red onslaught'.

Dien Cecht: The great medicine man of the Tuatha Dé Danann.

Dindsenchus: Literally, 'place lore'.

Dionysus: The Greek god of wine.

Divine Ground or *Divine Ungrund*: A German mystical term denoting the divine no-ground that grounds.

Druidheacht: Literally, 'magic'.

Eagla Fhinn: Fear of Fionn or, more generally perhaps, fear of authority.

Ecumene: A world in which all things live ecumenically with all things.

Éire: The goddess of Irish sovereignty and of the land of Ireland in one of her three distinct manifestations. Here she represents a distinct dimension of the land of Ireland. See *Banbha* and *Fódhla*.

Emain Abhlach: A name of the Celtic Otherworld, the Avalon to which the wounded King Arthur returns for healing.

Emuin Macha: Navan fort in Armagh.

Énflaith: A compound of two Irish words, 'én', meaning 'bird', and 'flaith', meaning 'reign', hence 'birdreign'. In early, semi-mythically imagined Irish history, the reign of King Conaire Mór, during which all things lived ecumenically with all things. Here we propose an Énflaith, not a republic.

Eó fis i llind: The all-wise, all-knowing salmon in a pool of the river Boyne called Linn Feic or, for that matter, in any pool of any river. See *Linn Feic*.

Étain: A tragic heroine in Irish myth.

Fál: The Stone of Destiny on the Hill of Tara, County Meath.

Fand: The wife of Manannán mac Lir.

Fidchel: An old Irish board game. Whether it bore much resemblance to chess or draughts we cannot say.

Fintan mac Bochra (or sometimes *Bóchna*): Literally, 'Fintan, son of the Sea'. The first name, Fintan, suggests that he is old, white-haired and wise. Among the first settlers in Ireland, he lived for centuries, transmigrating from one to another shape, from a salmon in Lough Derg to a hawk in Achill, the result being that, having observed it all, he knew the whole history of Ireland.

Fír Flathemon: The ontological and moral truth and justice of a ruler.

Fisher King, the: The sexually wounded keeper of the Holy Grail. In consequence of his impotence his entire kingdom is a wasteland. Seeking distraction from his agony he will sometimes go fishing from a boat under his castle, that is the Grail castle. Often, it is in this guise that a questing knight will first see him. Hence the name by which he is most widely known.

Foclut Wood: A wood in north-west Mayo from which and from the environs of which St Patrick, back again in England, heard a people he had once lived with calling him back among them.

Fódhla: The goddess of Irish sovereignty and of the land of Ireland in one of her three distinct manifestations. In this book she represents a distinct dimension of the land of Ireland. See *Banbha* and *Éire*.

Fomorians: In the mythical imagination of the Irish, a terrible spectral people who live on islands on the western ocean and harrass and invade Ireland. Here they are also the antitype of ourselves, which we are constantly in danger of becoming.

Foras Feasa ar Éirinn: A book by Seathrún Céitinn (*c*. 1580–1644). In itself, the title suggests an in-depth, historical understanding of Ireland.

Gaiakhty: The Earth coming up over its own karmic horizon.

Ginunngagap: In Norse mythology, the great yawning void before and after worlds.

Gopi: In Hindu tradition, a passionate female devotee of Lord Krishna, an avatar or incarnation of the great god Vishnu.

Gotterdammerung: A German word literally meaning 'the twilight of the gods'. The doom of the gods, signifying the end of the world. See *Ragnarok*.

Hawk's Well: In his book *The History and Topography of Ireland* Gerald of Wales says: 'There is a well of sweet water in Connacht on the top of a high mountain and some distance from the sea, which in any one day ebbs and overflows three times, imitating the ebbing and flowing of the sea.' This is the Hawk's Well on Tullaghan Hill near Coolaney in County Sligo, and not only is its water sometimes bitter like sea water, it is sometimes sweet like ordinary water. *At the Hawk's Well* is the title of a famous play by W.B. Yeats, in which Cú Chulainn finds his destiny as a warrior.

Huitzilopochtli: The chief Aztec god – sungod, wargod – to whom, in the literal sense, actual human hearts were offered.

Iath nAnann: Literally, 'the land of the goddess Danu' (*q.v.*).

Idumea: A territory in biblical lands. See Isaiah 34:5–15.

Imram Brain: Literally, 'Bran's rowing about the sea'. The voyage during which Manannán mac Lir, god of the sea, sang to him.

In Tenga Bithnua: Literally, 'the ever-new tongue'. The name of an early Irish Christian text of which John Carey says that 'it sees the vastness and the intricacy of the universe as an adumbration of the glory of God'.

Ind Énflaith: Literally, 'the Birdreign'. In early Ireland the reign of King Conaire Mór was known as the Birdreign, when all things lived ecumenically with all things. See *Conaire Mór* and *Énflaith*.

Inis Dairbhre: Valencia Island, off the coast of County Kerry.

Jnana Yoga: The practice of using our mind to go beyond mind in our quest for union with God.

Kedron: The stream that Jesus crossed en route to Gethsemane.

Labby Rock: A dolmen quite near Magh Tuired in County Sligo, site of the great battle between the forces of good and evil. The word 'labby' comes from 'leaba', the Irish word for 'bed'. All dolmens, including this one, were regarded as the love-beds of Diarmaid and Gráinne.

Lia Fáil: See *Fál*.

Liebestod: A German word meaning 'love-death'.

Linn Feic: The pool in the river Boyne in which the god as all-wise salmon lives. See *Eó fis i llind*.

Lughnasadh: The name of the harvest festival in honour of the god Lugh. It is also the Irish name for the entire month of August.

Maat: In ancient Egyptian religion, the goddess of truth, and cosmic and social right order.

Macha: The Irish name of the Celtic horse goddess. In Welsh she is called Rhiannon; the continental Celts know her as Epona.

Máel Dúin: The hero of a famous old Irish story called 'Immram Curaig Moile Dúin', 'The Voyage of Máel Dúin's Currach'. Drawn back into it as he and his men set sail for home, Máel Dúin himself remained in the Otherworld. His men made it home.

Magh Meall: Literally 'Plain of Delights'. A paradisal Otherworld in Irish mythology.

Magh Tuired: The site, thought to be in County Sligo, of a great battle between the Fomorians and the Tuatha Dé Danann. Literally, the 'Plain of Pillars', perhaps the 'Plain of Standing Stones'. As the great archetypal battle between the forces of light and darkness, the Battle of Magh Tuired has its equivalent among many Indo-European peoples.

Mahavakya: A Sanskrit word meaning 'a great saying'.

Mahadeviyaka: A Hindu saint, or bhakta (*q.v.*) of the twelfth century from southern India. She testified in poem after poem to her passionate devotion to the god Shiva.

Manannán mac Lir: In Irish mythology, Manannán, son of the Sea, god of the sea.

Metanoesis: Compound of two Greek words, 'meta' and 'noesis', meaning 'beyond mental activity', 'beyond thinking'. As the Chandogya Upanishad has it: 'Where nothing else is seen, nothing else is heard, nothing else is thought about, there is Divine Plenitude.'

Milesian: A mythological invader, one of the first to inhabit the land of Ireland.

Mirum: A thing of wonder.

Nemtenga: The bitter or poisonous tongue.

Nine waves: The nine waves, suggesting the waves of an agate, that immediately surround Ireland. Their tradition of meaning continuing to elude us, here they are the nine initiations into wonder preparing us for the wonder of the land itself.

Ogma: One of the great heroes of the Tuatha Dé Danann.

Ollamh Fódhla: A teacher and legislator out of a dimension of Ireland called Fódhla. The questions we ask here are how in our day would someone become such a teacher and what would they have to teach and what as legislator would they establish, a republic or an Énflaith? On the basis that each of us is nightly a salmon in a pool, surely an Énflaith?

Orpheus: The great Greek singer.

Paps of Danu: See *Dá Chích Danann*.

Paps of Morrigu: See *Dá Chích na Morrígna*.

Partholon: A mythological invader, one of the first to inhabit the land of Ireland.

Paschal Candle: A candle with five nails in it, representing the five wounds of Christ.

Poll na Brón: A dolmen in the Burren in County Clare.

Radha: Being the most passionate of the gopis, she is the favourite of Lord Krishna. See *Gopi*.

Ragnarok: Norse word suggesting the doom of the gods and with it the cataclysmic end of the world. See *Gotterdammerung*.

River of the White Hippopotamus: In ancient Egyptian myth one of the great rivers of the Underworld.

Saighir, Seir: Site of a monastery in County Offaly.

Sambhogakaya: The bliss body in Buddhism.

Samhain: November the first, beginning of the Celtic year.

Satori: In Zen Buddhism, a moment of arrest in final in-sight.

Scathách: A warrior queen who lived in Scotland and who taught Cú Chulainn many seemingly impossible feats of arms.

Scelec: The old name of Skellig Michael, a holy island off the County Kerry coastline.

Shantih: Literally, 'peace', a word repeated at the end of an Upanishad.

Sheela-na-gig: A goddess or spook who, bringing her hands forward between her thighs from behind, holds her vast vulva open. She can still be seen, carved in high or in low relief, in some old Christian churches. There are women who, to this day, will seek a remedy for infertility by touching the gaping vulva with an handkerchief and blessing themselves with it.

Sidh ar Feimhin: The cairn or the summit of Slievenamon in County Tipperary, said to be the home of Bodhbh Dearg, of the Tuatha Dé Danann and the King of Munster.

Silver branch: The marvellous way of seeing and knowing things that Manannán mac Lir, god of the sea, sent into the world. It came among us in the form of an actual singing silver branch, or as Hindus might say, in the form of an actual om-sounding silver branch.

Silver-branch perception: In biblical terms, paradisal perception or, more boldly, the marvellous way of seeing and knowing things that, in effect, is paradise regained. In his poem, 'The Marriage of Heaven and Hell', William Blake says: 'If the doors of perception were cleansed every thing would appear to man as it is, infinite.' Silver-branch perception is in all ways the opposite of our Súil Mildagach way of seeing and knowing. See Thomas Traherne's famous 'Century', beginning, 'The corn was orient and immortal wheat …'

Slieve Mish: Mountain above Tralee in County Kerry.

Súil Mildagach: Balar's poison eye. See *Balar's evil eye*.

Sutra: A religious-philosophical text, of which there are many, believed to have been spoken by the Buddha. Among the most famous of them are the Diamond Sutra, the Heart Sutra, the Lankavatara Sutra and the Lotus of the Good Law.

Tailtiu: In County Meath, adjacent to the river Boyne.

Táin Bó Cuailnge: The name of an Irish epic that describes the efforts of a queen and her army to steal a famous bull. The Irish word 'táin' means 'cattle raid', usually conducted across tribal boundaries in ancient and medieval Ireland.

Tao Te Ching: A religious-philosophical Chinese text said to have been composed by Lao Tzu.

Tezcatlipoca: Aztec god of night whose name means 'Smoking Mirror'.

Tír Tairngrí: The Celtic Otherworld, having specific reference to the marvellous world where Manannán mac Lir, god of the sea, lives.

Toraíocht: Literally, 'pursuit' (of Diarmuid and Gráinne).

Torc Mountain: Near Killarney in County Kerry.

Tuatha Dé Danann: The euhemerized gods of the ancient Irish, traditionally thought of as a distinct race of people who once inhabited the land and who, after their defeat by the Gaels, went underground into the hollow hills from where, if properly recognized and regarded, they guarantee the fertility of the land.

Uaigh na gCat: A cave in Cruachan, County Roscommon. To Pagans it was an entrance to the Otherworld. To Christians it was the mouth of hell. At Samhain every year three terrible feline terrors emerged from it. Hence its name, the 'Cave of the Cats'.

Uisnech: The centre of Ireland, the fifth province (located in County Westmeath).

Upanishad: A mystical Hindu text, of which there are more than a hundred having canonical status.

Urizen: A negative, eyeblighted, mind-blighted and therefore world-blighting figure in Blake's mythic imagination.

Vajrasatvically: A compound of two Sanskrit words, 'vajra' meaning 'thunderbolt' and 'sat' meaning 'being' or 'a being'. A being of the highest ontological order. A being as real and as indestructible as the thunderbolt. Morally and ontologically, a diamond being.

Wolf-Time: In a Norse poem 'Voluspo', which describes the cataclysmic end of the world, we read:

> Brothers shall fight and fell each other,
> And sister's sons shall kinship stain;
> Hard is the earth with nightly whoredom;
> Axe-time, sword-time, shields are sundered,
> Wind-time, wolf-time, ere the world falls,
> Nor ever shall men each other spare ...

Xipe Totec: The Aztec god of fertility.

Yggdrasil: In Scandinavian mythology, the world-ash, the tree in whose branches and roots are nine worlds.

Select Bibliography

Carey, John, *King of Mysteries* (Dublin: Four Courts Press 1998).

D'arbois de Jusoinville, H., '*Talies in and Amairgen': The Irish Mythological Cycle* (Dublin: O'Donoghue and Company 1903).

Dillon, Myles (ed.), *Serlige Con Culainn* (Dublin: The Dublin Institute for Advanced Studies 1975).

Eckhart, Meister, *A Modern Translation*, translated by Raymond Bernard Blakney (New York: Harper Torchbooks 1941).

Eliade, Mircea, *The Voluspo: From Primitive to Zen* (London: William Collins, Sons and Company 1967).

Flower, Robin, *The Irish Tradition* (Dublin: The Lilliput Press 1994).

Foster, R.F., *The Irish Story* (London: Penguin Books 2001).

Gray, Elizabeth A. (ed.), *Cath Maige Tuiread* (Dublin: Irish Texts Society 1982).

Holy Bible, The (authorized King James version 1611).

Hughes, Ted, *The Collected Poems*, edited by Paul Keegan (London: Faber and Faber 2003).

Knott, Eleanor (ed.), *Togail Bruidne Dá Derga* (Dublin: The Dublin Institute for Advanced Studies 1975).

Law, William, *Characters and Characteristics of William Law*, selected and arranged by Alexander Whyte, D.D. (London: Hodder and Stoughton 1989).

Lawrence, D.H., *The Complete Poems*, edited by Vivian De Sola Pinto and Warren Roberts (London: Penguin 1993).

Muir, Edwin, *Collected Poems*, second edition (London: Faber and Faber 1985).

Murphy, Gerard (ed.), 'Poems 5, 6 and 51', *Early Irish Lyrics* (Dublin: Four Courts Press 1998).

Ní Sheaghdha, Ness (ed.), *Tóruigheacht Dhiarmada agus Ghráinne* (Dublin: Irish Texts Society 1967).

Ó Tuama, Seán, *An Dunaire 1600–1900: Poems of the Dispossessed.* Translations by Thomas Kinsella (Dublin: The Dolmen Press 1981).

Porete, Marguerite, *A Mirror for Simple Souls*, edited, translated and adapted by Charles Crawford (Dublin: Gill and Macmillan 1981).

Ramanujan, A.K., *Speaking of Shiva* (London: Penguin Books 1973).

Thomas, Dylan, *Collected Poems* (London: J.M. Dent and Sons 1952).

Underhill, Evelyn, *Henry Suso: Mysticism* (London: Methuen and Company 1911).

Yeats, W.B., *Autobiographies* (Dublin: Gill and Macmillan 1955).

Zaehner, R.C. (ed.), *'The Bhagavad Gita': Hindu Scriptures* (London: J.M. Dent and Sons 1996).

JOHN MORIARTY was born in North Kerry in 1938 and educated at Listowel and University College Dublin. He taught English Literature at the University of Manitoba in Canada for six years, before returning to Ireland in 1971. In June 2006 he received an honorary degree (D.Litt.) from the National University of Ireland, Galway.

He is the author of *Dreamtime* (1994, revised 1999), the trilogy *Turtle Was Gone a Long Time: Crossing the Kedron* (1996), *Horsehead Nebula Neighing* (1997) and *Anaconda Canoe* (1998), *Nostos, an autobiography* (2001) and *Night Journey to Buddh Gaia* (forthcoming, 2006).